SOUTHERN CALIFORNIA NATURE GUIDE

Erin McCloskey

with contributions from

Andy Bezener, Krista Kagume & Linda Kershaw

Lone Pine Publishing

Distributed by Lone Pine Publishing
10145–81 Avenue
Edmonton, AB T6E 1W9
Canada

Website: www.lonepinepublishing.com

Publisher's Cataloging-In-Publication Data
(Prepared by The Donohue Group, Inc.)

McCloskey, Erin, 1970-
   Southern California nature guide / Erin McCloskey.

   p. : col. ill., col. maps ; cm.

   Includes bibliographical references and index.
   ISBN-13: 978-976-8200-55-6
   ISBN-10: 976-8200-55-3

1. Natural history—California, Southern—Guidebooks. 2. Nature study—California, Southern—Guidebooks. 3. California, Southern—Guidebooks. 4. Animals—Identification. 5. Plants—Identification. I. Title.

QH105.C2 M33 2009   508.7/949

Cover Illustrations: Frank Burman, spreading phlox & California flannel bush; Ted Nordhagen, western scrub-jay & American kestrel; Gary Ross, mule deer; Ian Sheldon, gray whale, gulf fritillary, green darner & short-beaked common dolphin. *Illustrations:* please see p. 4 for a complete list of credits

Disclaimer: This guide is not intended to be a "how to" reference guide for food or medicinal uses of plants. We do not recommend experimentation by readers, and we caution that a number of woody plants in Southern California, including some used traditionally as medicines, are poisonous and harmful.

PC: 15

TABLE OF CONTENTS

ILLUSTRATION CREDITS

Frank Burman: 121a, 144c, 153a, 153b, 154, 155, 156, 157, 158, 159, 160a, 160c, 161, 162, 163, 166, 167a, 168a, 169b, 169c, 170a, 171, 172, 173a, 174a, 175e, 176b, 177, 180, 181b, 181c, 182, 183, 184, 185, 186c, 187c, 188f, 189, 190, 191, 192c, 193a, 193c, 194a, 194c, 195a, 196, 197

Ivan Droujinin: 120, 124a, 125a, 127b, 127c

Kindrie Grove: 73c

Linda Kershaw: 175d

Ted Nordhagen: 90b, 91a, 92, 93a, 94a, 96a, 98, 99b, 101a, 103c, 104, 106a, 107b, 107c, 108, 109, 110a, 111a, 111b, 112b, 113a, 114b, 115a, 115c, 117a, 117b, 118

Gary Ross: 48, 49, 50, 51, 52, 53, 54, 60b, 61b, 62, 63, 64, 65, 66, 67, 68, 69, 70, 71, 72, 73a, 73b, 74, 75, 78, 79, 80, 81, 82, 83, 84, 85, 86, 87, 88, 89, 90a, 91b, 93b, 93c, 94b, 94c, 95, 96b, 96c, 97, 99a, 99c, 100, 101b, 101c, 102, 103a, 103b, 105, 106b, 106c, 107a, 110b, 111c, 112a, 112c, 113b, 113c, 114a, 114c, 115b, 116, 117c, 121b, 121c, 122a, 122b, 123, 125a, 126, 127a

Ian Sheldon: 55, 56, 57, 58, 59, 60a, 61a, 124b, 125c, 129, 130, 131, 134, 135, 136, 137, 138, 139, 140, 141, 142, 144a, 144b, 145, 146, 147, 148, 149, 150, 153c, 153d, 160b, 166, 167b, 167c, 168b, 168c, 169a, 170b, 170c, 170d, 173b, 173c, 174b, 174c, 174d, 174e, 175a, 175b, 175c, 176a, 181a, 186a, 187a, 187b, 188a, 188b, 188c, 188d, 188e, 192a, 192b, 193b, 194b, 195b, 195c, 198, 199

DEDICATION

This one is for you, Mom! For being close at heart even when I am living far away.

ACKNOWLEDGMENTS

Thanks to all the authors of previous Lone Pine texts who have created such a great library of background information, namely Krista Kagume, Tamara Eder, Ian Sheldon and John Acorn, as well as Andy Bezener and Linda Kershaw, with whom I had the pleasure of working on the first of this nature guide series, the *Rocky Mountain Nature Guide*.

Special thanks to the following people for their assistance in the development of the species lists: Maddalena Bearzi (President and Co-founder of the Ocean Conservation Society), Brian Brown (Natural History Museum of Los Angeles County, Entomology), Gary M. Langham (Director of Bird Conservation Audubon California), John Malpas (Calflora) and Ken Gilliland.

MAMMALS

American Bison
p. 48

Bighorn Sheep
p. 48

Elk
p. 49

Mule Deer
p. 49

Pronghorn
p. 50

Feral Horse
p. 50

Feral Pig
p. 51

American Black Bear
p. 51

Mountain Lion
p. 52

Bobcat
p. 52

Coyote
p. 53

Gray Fox
p. 53

Kit Fox
p. 54

Red Fox
p. 54

Gray Whale
p. 55

Minke Whale
p. 55

Fin Whale
p. 56

Humpback Whale
p. 56

Blue Whale
p. 57

Orca
p. 57

Bottlenose Dolphin
p. 58

Short-beaked Common Dolphin
p. 58

Risso's Dolphin
p. 59

Pacific White-sided Dolphin
p. 59

Northern Elephant Seal
p. 60

Harbor Seal
p. 60

California Sea-lion
p. 61

Sea Otter
p. 61

American Marten
p. 62

Long-tailed Weasel
p. 62

Badger
p. 62

Striped Skunk
p. 63

Western Spotted Skunk
p. 63

MAMMALS

Ringtail
p. 64

Raccoon
p. 64

Porcupine
p. 65

Beaver
p. 65

Common Muskrat
p. 66

Desert Woodrat
p. 66

Desert Kangaroo Rat
p. 66

Norway Rat
p. 67

House Mouse
p. 67

Deer Mouse
p. 67

California Vole
p. 68

Long-tailed Pocket Mouse
p. 68

Botta's Pocket Gopher
p. 68

California Ground Squirrel
p. 69

Merriam's Chipmunk
p. 69

Western Gray Squirrel
p. 69

White-tailed Antelope Squirrel
p. 70

Northern Flying Squirrel
p. 70

Black-tailed Jackrabbit
p. 70

Brush Rabbit
p. 71

Desert Cottontail
p. 71

Brazilian Free-tailed Bat
p. 71

Western Mastiff Bat
p. 72

Little Brown Bat
p. 72

Hoary Bat
p. 72

Western Pipistrelle
p. 73

Big Brown Bat
p. 73

Pallid Bat
p. 73

Townsend's Big-eared Bat
p. 74

California Leaf-nosed Bat
p. 74

Broad-footed Mole
p. 74

Ornate Shrew
p. 75

Virginia Opossum
p. 75

Canada Goose
p. 78

Mallard
p. 78

Northern Pintail
p. 79

BIRDS

Cinnamon Teal
p. 79

Northern Shoveler
p. 80

American Wigeon
p. 80

Lesser Scaup
p. 81

Surf Scoter
p. 81

Bufflehead
p. 82

Red-breasted Merganser
p. 82

Ruddy Duck
p. 83

California Quail
p. 83

Pacific Loon
p. 84

Pied-billed Grebe
p. 84

Eared Grebe
p. 84

Western Grebe
p. 85

Brown Pelican
p. 85

Double-crested Cormorant
p. 85

Great Blue Heron
p. 86

Great Egret
p. 86

Snowy Egret
p. 86

Black-crowned Night-heron
p. 87

Turkey Vulture
p. 87

California Condor
p. 87

White-tailed Kite
p. 88

Northern Harrier
p. 88

Cooper's Hawk
p. 89

Red-shouldered Hawk
p. 89

Red-tailed Hawk
p. 90

American Kestrel
p. 90

Sora
p. 91

American Coot
p. 91

Black-bellied Plover
p. 92

Killdeer
p. 92

Black-necked Stilt
p. 92

American Avocet
p. 93

Greater Yellowlegs
p. 93

Willet
p. 93

Black Turnstone
p. 94

BIRDS

Sanderling
p. 94

Western Sandpiper
p. 94

Dunlin
p. 95

Wilson's Snipe
p. 95

Heerman's Gull
p. 96

Ring-billed Gull
p. 96

California Gull
p. 96

Western Gull
p. 97

Caspian Tern
p. 97

Forster's Tern
p. 97

Least Tern
p. 98

Black Skimmer
p. 98

Rock Pigeon
p. 99

Mourning Dove
p. 99

Greater Roadrunner
p. 99

Barn Owl
p. 100

Great Horned Owl
p. 100

White-throated Swift
p. 100

Anna's Hummingbird
p. 101

Allen's Hummingbird
p. 101

Belted Kingfisher
p. 101

Acorn Woodpecker
p. 102

Nuttall's Woodpecker
p. 102

Northern Flicker
p. 102

Black Phoebe
p. 103

Pacific-slope Flycatcher
p. 103

Western Kingbird
p. 103

Warbling Vireo
p. 104

Western Scrub-Jay
p. 104

American Crow
p. 105

Common Raven
p. 105

Horned Lark
p. 106

Tree Swallow
p. 106

Cliff Swallow
p. 106

Oak Titmouse
p. 107

Wrentit
p. 107

BIRDS

Bushtit
p. 107

Pygmy Nuthatch
p. 108

Bewick's Wren
p. 108

Ruby-crowned Kinglet
p. 108

Blue-gray Gnatcatcher
p. 109

Western Bluebird
p. 109

Hermit Thrush
p. 109

American Robin
p. 110

Northern Mockingbird
p. 110

European Starling
p. 111

Cedar Waxwing
p. 111

Orange-crowned Warbler
p. 111

Yellow Warbler
p. 112

Yellow-rumped Warbler
p. 112

Townsend's Warbler
p. 112

Common Yellowthroat
p. 113

Wilson's Warbler
p. 113

Western Tanager
p. 113

California Towhee
p. 114

Savannah Sparrow
p. 114

Song Sparrow
p. 114

White-crowned Sparrow
p. 115

Dark-eyed Junco
p. 115

Black-headed Grosbeak
p. 115

Red-winged Blackbird
p. 116

Western Meadowlark
p. 116

Brewer's Blackbird
p. 116

Brown-headed Cowbird
p. 117

Bullock's Oriole
p. 117

House Finch
p. 117

American Goldfinch
p. 118

Lazuli Bunting
p. 118

House Sparrow
p. 118

California Newt
p. 120

California Tiger Salamander
p. 120

Western Spadefoot
p. 121

Western Toad
p. 121

Bullfrog
p. 121

Red-legged Frog
p. 122

AMPHIBIANS & REPTILES

Pacific Treefrog
p. 122

Western Painted Turtle
p. 123

Western Pond Turtle
p. 123

Desert Tortoise
p. 123

Southern Alligator Lizard
p. 124

Sagebrush Lizard
p. 124

Western Fence Lizard
p. 125

Western Whiptail
p. 125

Western Skink
p. 125

Yellow-bellied Racer
p. 126

Western Rattlesnake
p. 126

Common Gartersnake
p. 126

Gophersnake
p. 127

Kingsnake
p. 127

California Whipsnake
p. 127

FISH

Cutthroat Trout
p. 129

Rainbow Trout
p. 129

Brook Trout
p. 129

FISH

Black Prickleback
p. 130

Blackeye Goby
p. 130

Longjaw Mudsucker
p. 130

Wooly Sculpin
p. 131

Grunion
p. 131

Round Stingray
p. 131

INVERTEBRATES

Giant Owl Limpet
p. 134

Black Abalone
p. 134

Black Tegula
p. 134

California Mussel
p. 135

Lined Chiton
p. 135

Bean Clam
p. 135

Opalescent Nudibranch
p. 136

Dwarf Sea Cucumber
p. 136

Bat Star
p. 136

Ochre Sea Star
p. 137

Eccentric Sand Dollar
p. 137

Purple Sea Urchin
p. 137

Aggregating Anemone
p. 138

Giant Green Anemone
p. 138

Orange Cup Coral
p. 138

Purple Sponge
p. 139

Sea Gooseberry
p. 139

Opalescent Squid
p. 139

Giant Acorn Barnacle
p. 140

Red Rock Shrimp
p. 140

California Beach Flea
p. 140

Striped Shore Crab
p. 141

Blue-handed Hermit Crab
p. 141

California Spiny Lobster
p. 141

Western Tiger Swallowtail
p. 142

Monarch
p. 142

Gulf Fritillary
p. 142

West Coast Lady
p. 143

California Sister
p. 143

Mourning Cloak
p. 143

Snowberry Clearwing
p. 144

White-lined Sphinx
p. 144

Black Witch
p. 144

Boreal Bluet
p. 145

Green Darner
p. 145

Variegated Meadowhawk
p. 145

Yellow Jackets
p. 146

Bumble Bees
p. 146

Carpenter Bees
p. 146

Convergent Ladybug
p. 147

INVERTEBRATES

Carpenter Ants
p. 147

Crane Flies
p. 147

Cicada
p. 148

Jerusalem Cricket
p. 148

California Mantid
p. 148

German Cockroach
p. 149

Scorpion
p. 149

Golden Orb Weaver
p. 149

California Ebony Tarantula
p. 150

Western Black Widow
p. 150

TREES

White Fir
p. 153

Shore Pine
p. 153

Jeffrey Pine
p. 154

Sugar Pine
p. 154

Yellow Pine
p. 155

Pinyon Pine
p. 155

Monterey Cypress
p. 156

Incense Cedar
p. 156

Giant Sequoia
p. 157

Tanoak
p. 157

California Live Oak
p. 158

Coastal Scrub Oak
p. 158

Cottonwood
p. 159

Pacific Madrone
p. 159

Big-leaf Maple
p. 160

California Boxelder
p. 160

California Laurel
p. 161

Blue Palo Verde
p. 161

California Fan Palm
p. 162

Joshua Tree
p. 162

Eucalyptus
p. 163

California Buckeye
p. 163

Junipers
p. 166

Prince's-pine
p. 166

Common Bearberry
p. 166

Manzanita
p. 167

Scouler's Willow
p. 167

Desert Willow
p. 168

Red-osier Dogwood
p. 168

Western Serviceberry
p. 169

Mountain Mahogany
p. 169

Island Ironwood Tree
p. 169

Toyon
p. 170

Thimbleberry
p. 170

Ninebark
p. 170

Oceanspray
p. 171

Shrubby Cinquefoil
p. 171

Bitterbrush
p. 171

Chamise
p. 172

Scotch Broom
p. 172

Desert Ironwood
p. 172

Coyote Brush
p. 173

Sagebrush
p. 173

Rabbitbush
p. 173

California Lilacs
p. 174

Common Snowberry
p. 174

SHRUBS

Twinberry
p. 174

Elderberry
p. 175

Poison Oak
p. 175

Skunkbrush
p. 176

Creeping Barberry
p. 176

Creosote Bush
p. 177

California Flannel Bush
p. 177

HERBS, FERNS, CACTI, SUCCULENTS & SEAWEEDS

California False-hellebore
p. 180

Death Camas
p. 180

Miner's Lettuce
p. 180

Field Chickweed
p. 181

American Winter Cress
p. 181

Field Mustard
p. 181

Milk Maids
p. 182

Peppergrass
p. 182

California Poppy
p. 182

Pacific Bleeding Heart
p. 183

Small-flowered Woodland Star
p. 183

Brook Saxifrage
p. 183

Pacific Sedum
p. 184

Windflower
p. 184

Western Columbine
p. 184

Marsh Marigold
p. 185

Buttercup
p. 185

Meadowrue
p. 185

Beach Strawberry
p. 186

Apache Plume
p. 186

Violets
p. 186

Broadleaf Lupine
p. 187

Clovers
p. 187

Winter Vetch
p. 187

Fireweed & California Fuschias
p. 188

Cow Parsnip
p. 188

Northern Gentian
p. 189

Western Waterleaf
p. 189

Baby Blue-eyes
p. 189

Lacy Phacelia
p. 190

Spreading Phlox
p. 190

Toothed Downingia
p. 190

Pennyroyal
p. 191

Woolly Bluecurls
p. 191

White Sage
p. 191

Scarlet Paintbrush
p. 192

Yellow Monkeyflower
p. 192

Penstemon
p. 192

American Brooklime
p. 193

Common Yarrow
p. 193

23

HERBS, FERNS, CACTI, SUCCULENTS & SEAWEEDS

Leafy Aster
p. 193

Brass Buttons
p. 194

Fleabane
p. 194

Common Tarweed
p. 194

Woolly Mule Ears
p. 195

Goldenrod
p. 195

Sulphur Buckwheat
p. 195

Bracken Fern
p. 196

Sword Fern
p. 196

Maidenhair Fern
p. 196

Desert Agave
p. 197

Prickly Pear Cactus
p. 197

Winterfat
p. 197

Surf Grass & Eel Grass
p. 198

Turkish Towel
p. 198

Giant Kelp
p. 199

Bull Kelp
p. 199

Sea Lettuce
p. 199

Those of you who have picked up this guide in appreciation and recognition of the natural beauty of Southern California, and who are interested in more than just Hollywood and Disneyland, may already be familiar with many of the species of plants and animals discussed in these pages; or perhaps you are about to see them for the first time. Whether you are a California dreamer visiting the state or one of the lucky residents enjoying California living, there is always a new plant, animal or natural area to discover; some species are widespread beyond California's borders, whereas many others are found nowhere else in the world but here. California has one of the highest number of endemic species in North America owing to an incredible range of habitat formed by unique combinations of geology, climate, elevation, latitude and ocean currents. Marine and coastal zones, the Channel Islands, several mountain ranges, two deserts, chaparral, Joshua tree woodlands, sagebrush scrublands and pinyon-pine/juniper and oak woodlands create a dramatic variety of landscapes that contribute to the scenic beauty and distinct ecology of Southern California.

In the bays and inlets along our coastline, we can see abundant marine life, and we are frequently delighted by the sight of whales passing by just offshore. American black bears and mountain lions still roam in protected, remote areas, reminding us that parts of California remain truly wild. Coyotes, deer, foxes, hawks, songbirds, bats, butterflies, frogs and snakes bring the "wild" right into our cities; even those animals that some may consider pests, such as pigeons, house sparrows and several insects species, with a slight shift in our attitude, allow us to appreciate the diversity of life within what would otherwise be a lonely, single species, urban setting. Bugs are also wildlife, and there are more than 20,000 species of insects to be observed throughout the state. California is extremely varied with several different bioregions and ecoregions. Looking at these natural regions can lead to a better understanding of the plants and animals living there and how they interact with each other.

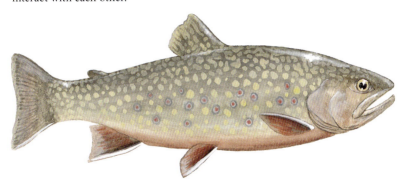

ECOREGIONS OF SOUTHERN CALIFORNIA

THE PACIFIC OCEAN, ISLANDS AND MAINLAND COAST

The Pacific Ocean offers open-sea habitat for pelagic seabirds, marine mammals and deep-sea marine life to thrill divers, sport fishers, birdwatchers and whale watchers; sea-shell strewn sands keep beachcombers entertained along the jagged, rocky coastline, which the surf nibbles away to create bays, inlets, lagoons and innumerable tide pools teeming with life.

The Channel Islands

This island chain includes the five islands of the Channel Island National Park (San Miguel, Santa Rosa, Santa Cruz, Anacapa and Santa Barbara; see more below) as well as three southern islands: Santa Catalina, San Clements and San Nicolas. They are a seaward extension of the Santa Monica Mountains and are believed to have separated from the mainland during the Pleistocene Ice Age, which began about one and a half million years ago. Four of the northern islands were connected approximately 18,000 years ago as a single island called Santarosae. Many species found on the Channel Islands are endemic, such as the island fox, which is related to the mainland gray fox but is about the size of a house cat. Sixty-five plant species do not exist anywhere else in the world but on these islands.

The Santa Barbara Channel

There are a few important marine currents and upwellings off the California coast that affect water temperatures and conditions, in turn influencing which species can live there. Near-shore cold and warm currents vary somewhat in temperature each year, influencing species diversity, such as prey availability for many species including coastal-breeding cormorants and western gulls. El Niño–Southern Oscillation events greatly influence the number of subtropical wintering migrants in our area.

The deep waters of the clockwise-turning North Pacific Subtropical Gyre beyond the continental slope are

Ecoregions of California

Marine West Coast Forest
 Coast Range

Mediterranean California
California Coastal Sage, Chaparral and Oak Woodlands

Central California Valley

Southern and Baja California Pine-Oak Mountains

Western Cordillera
Sierra Nevada

Klamath Mountains

Eastern Cascades Slopes and Foothills

Cascades

Cold Deserts
Northern Basin and Range

Central Basin and Range

Warm Deserts
Mojave Basin and Range

Sonoran Desert

27

generally fairly warm throughout the year (from the perspective of large, blubbery mammals such as whales), moving warmer southern waters to the north. One of the four prevailing ocean currents that comprise the gyre is the large offshore California current, which moves cold arctic waters south to Northern California's shores, making the water quite chilly for us humans. However, the coast of Southern California is tucked into the Santa Monica Bay, where the Southern California Countercurrent carries warm water back up north through the Santa

Barbara Channel, between the mainland and the Channel Islands. These warmer waters draw southern species into the region for the summer…and more bathers in for a swim…and create a marine biodiversity in Southern California that can be quite different from that of Central or Northern California. The two warm and cold Californian currents meet in the western section of the Santa Barbara Channel, which is within the Southern California Bight, bound in the north by Point Conception and in the south by Cape Colnett in Baja California, Mexico.

Point Conception

Point Conception, at the northern end of the Santa Barbara Channel and marked by the Point Conception Lighthouse, is considered the natural division between Southern and Central California. From this point, the coastline continues north in a more or less straight direction, whereas the coastline to the south veers to an east-west angle into the sheltered Santa Monica Bay along the Santa Barbara Channel and its warmer waters.

At this transition zone between cool northern waters and warm southern waters is one of earth's most biologically productive and biodiverse marine ecosystems; both southern and northern marine life can be found there. On San Miguel Island, an unprecedented six different species of seals and sea lions are found in the same waters and on the same beaches. The northern elephant seal's breeding grounds are around the Channel Islands; this animal is rarely seen south of Point Conception. Around the Southern California Bight, the blue whale has been recorded at its highest seasonal concentration of individuals worldwide.

Massive kelp forests provide habitat for numerous species of wildlife, including sea otters and sea urchins, and are a scuba diver's playground, famed worldwide. On the leeward side of Catalina Island are some of the best diving conditions in Southern California; this is the area where Jacques Cousteau filmed two episodes of his famous TV show *The Undersea World of Jacques Cousteau*—"Night of the Squid" and "Those Magnificent Diving Machines."

BRUSHLANDS, WOODLANDS, MOUNTAINS AND STEPPE
The Coastal Sage Scrub

This semi-arid zone runs along the coastal plains and valleys up to the slopes of the Santa Monica Mountains and south to San Diego, extending inland at low elevations to areas bordering the Mojave Desert. Shrubs with soft aromatic leaves, such as white sage, rely on surface moisture from the marine layer of fog during drought. Other plants typical of this zone are California buckwheat, brittle bush, manzanita and *Ceanothus* species, but California sagebrush and coyote brush are dominant and provide suitable habitat for animals such as the brush rabbit and goldfinch. Opossums are frequently seen in both natural and urban settings along the coast. A part of the Pacific flyway, California sees a great number of migratory birds along the coast in spring and fall, as well as insects—the most famous of all being the monarch. This zone intergrades with the chaparral zone.

The Chaparral

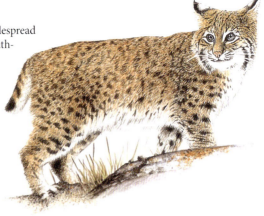

Chaparral is the most widespread plant community in Southern California. The shrubs are taller than in coastal scrub and are often in dense, thorny thickets. Chaparral, translated from the Spanish *el chaparro* meaning "place of small oak," is a type of scrub dwarf forest, too dry to support the true oak found at higher elevations. Evergreen shrubs such as *Ceanothus* species, manzanita, toyon, mountain mahogany and flannel bush are typical of this zone, and chamise is dominant because it is highly adapted to fire, which is a significant and common component of the chaparral, usually started by lightning (or by human carelessness) during the summer dry season. Fire is part of a natural cycle in this ecosystem, but because the chaparral is a zone that reaches into the highly human populated foothills of mountains such as the Santa Monica Mountains—part of which are more famously known as the Hollywood Hills—these fires can be devastating, resulting in a loss of personal property and sometimes loss of human life. Every year in Southern California tens of thousands of acres burn in these wildfires. The chaparral reaches decadence quickly with a fast, thick growth of dry plants that contain volatile oils and burn at least once every hundred years, despite great effort to prevent them from doing so. Fire allows for rejuvenation of plant growth, giving shade-intolerant species a chance to get a head start before the dense scrub returns, cracking open fire-dependant seeds allowing them to germinate, and releasing nutrients into the soil. Dense slow-growing wood and deep taproots save many of the tree-shrub species from being destroyed by the fires, surviving with only some charring that can be seen for years after the fire passed over them. With higher elevation and deeper soil, the chaparral transitions to foothill woodland (see below).

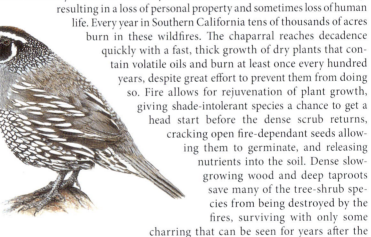

Sierran Steppe Coniferous and Mixed Forests

The southern reaches of the Sierra Nevada Range enter Southern California, sinking into the plains in Kern County. The semi-arid plant communities of low hills are evergreen chaparral, which give way to Sierran steppe coniferous and mixed forests with the typical Sierra conifer forests of various pines, white fir, sugar pine, yellow pine, Jeffrey pine, incense cedar and giant sequoia. The Sierra range is a long and remarkably tall uplift that vividly separates two entirely distinct climatic regimes in Central and Northern California. The long western slope of the Sierra Nevada rises gradually from 2000 to more than 14,000 feet. At 14,496 feet, Mt. Whitney is the crown of the Sierra bioregion and the highest mountain in the contiguous United States. The eastern slope drops abruptly to the floor of the Great Basin, about 4000 feet. Owing to its great range of elevation, its north-to-south extent and the meeting of "west-side" and "east-side" fauna and flora,

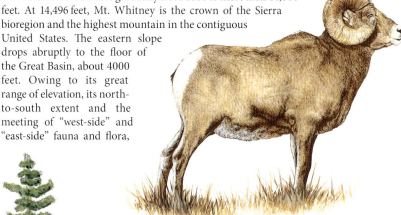

the Sierra Nevada Range is biologically complex. It boasts numerous state parks and national forests; Sequoia National Forest is in Kern County in Southern California. The oak and grassland habitats of the lower western slopes finger upward into scattered oak and pine woodlands across a broken but broad front. The lower eastern slopes support plants and animals that are characteristic of the fringes of the Great Basin (in the north) and the northern Mojave Desert (in the south). The diversity of plants in the Sierras is higher than in any other bio-region. The mountain wildflowers are spectacular and are acclaimed by all who are lucky enough to witness them in their full-blooming splendor. Like the plant diversity, the animal diversity in this bioregion is also very high; up to two-thirds of California's mammals can be found here. Bighorn sheep, mule deer, black bears, coyotes, red foxes, martens, porcupines and mountain lions are some of the most charismatic species, but other, smaller mammals are also abundant, including ground squirrels, woodrats and shrews. Birdlife includes yellow-rumped warblers, Cooper's hawks and great horned owls.

The Transverse Range and the Peninsular Range

Although the Sierra Nevadas barely dangle their feet into Southern California, two major mountain ranges are squarely within the area and govern the climate and biodiversity of this part of the state. The Transverse and Peninsular ranges are part of the North American Coast Range, which extends along the Pacific Coast

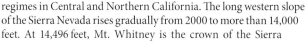

from Alaska to Mexico. The Transverse Range is named for its east-west direction change (which occurs at roughly Point Conception) that "transverses" the typically north-south direction of California's other ranges. The Transverse Range extends from the Channel Islands (which are the underwater extension of this range with the peaks above water forming islands) to the interior deserts (Mojave and Sonoran), separating the Mediterranean and the arid climates; the range includes several sets of smaller ranges, such as the Sierra Madre and Santa Ynez Mountains of Santa Barbara, the Santa Monica Mountains surrounding Los Angeles, the Santa Ana Mountains in Orange County and the San Gabriel Mountains to the east of Los Angeles, and it connects to the extensive San Bernardino Mountains, reaching out to the desert and the Cottonwood Mountains in Joshua Tree National Monument. The Peninsular Range extends from Palm Springs down through San Diego and includes the Santa Rosa and San Jacinto Mountains, among others. Both ranges are steep sloping to precipitous, with unstable slopes at elevation and sharp crests, and the valleys are narrow and sheltered, without harsh winters. The dramatic features of these ranges' profiles are a result of the collision of the plates along the infamous San Andreas Fault.

The Foothill Woodlands

In the lower elevations of both the Transverse Range and the Peninsular Range are the foothill woodlands, which include the southern oak woodlands. Here the shrub-dominant chaparral, mainly on south-facing slopes on drier sites, transitions to the tree-dominant sclerophyll forest—plants with tough, leathery evergreen foliage, mainly on north-facing slopes on wetter sites on hills and lower mountains. Some of the more common species in these woodlands are the California live oak, tanoak, California laurel and Pacific madrone, all of which are underscored with wildflowers. In drainage and riparian areas, shrubs include California buckeye and Scouler's willow.

Wildlife includes mule deer, coyotes, mountain lions, bobcats, gray foxes, wood rats, kangaroo rats and mice, spotted and striped skunks, Merriam chipmunks, wrentits, common bushtits, white-crowned sparrows, hermit thrushes, ruby-crowned kinglets, yellow-rumped warblers, California condors, gopher snakes and Pacific tree frogs.

32

Pinyon-Juniper Woodlands

At an elevation of about 3500 to 7000 feet, the pinyon-juniper woodlands mark the transition zone from mountains back down the eastern slopes and into the desert. This ecozone is found above the creosote bush scrub and Joshua tree woodland (see desert and semi-desert below) and below the pine/fir montane forests to the north. Pinyon pines and junipers dominate the woodland, but other shrubs such as mountain mahogany, rabbitbrush, sagebrush, scrub oak, flannel bush, and winterfat grow here among the yuccas and wildflowers, which include penstemon, buckwheat and Apache plume. Beckwick's wren, desert woodrat and Merriam's chipmunk, the latter of which relishes the pinyon pine nuts, are a few of the species found in this zone.

DESERT AND SEMI-DESERT

The dry climate zones, arid desert and transitional semi-arid steppe surrounding the desert are the most extensive on the planet, occupying roughly a quarter of the earth's land surface. There are no permanent streams in these zones, and the rate of evaporation is greater than that of precipitation, resulting in annual water deficit. No specific precipitation rate can be used to define a desert because temperature, elevation and latitude are variables that affect humidity and evaporation.

Creosote Bush Scrub

This hot desert plant community is where, as one would presume, creosote bush is the dominant plant species. Palo verde, desert ironwood, desert thorn, desert willow and *Opuntia* species are among the other plants that survive here in low densities. Plants adapted to arid environments often have silvery leaves that reflect sunlight, are turned on their edges to reduce exposure, are dormant in summer (growing and flowering in winter instead) and tend to rely on wind rather than animals for pollination.

Though vegetation and water are sparse and the climate is extreme, desert animals are well adapted to meet these demands. Desert animals can go without drinking, instead obtaining moisture from the seeds of plants, and they metabolize food and water very slowly to conserve these resources. Some species can concentrate their urine to conserve body water content and have nasal passages that can reabsorb the water vapor in their breath. Most desert species are nocturnal to avoid the heat of the sun and therefore often have big eyes.

The Mojave Desert

The Mojave Desert is a relatively high elevation (from sea level to 3900 feet) desert that transitions between the hot Sonoran and the cool Great Basin Joshua tree woodlands. Surrounding the desert at a higher elevation is the semi-desert; in Southern California along the edge of the Mojave Desert lies the Joshua tree woodland, which is well recognized and acclaimed for its iconic namesake. Death Valley is part of the Mojave Desert, where sand dunes, red rocks and salt flats comprise the starkly stunning landscape. The Joshua tree is an indicator species for the Mojave Desert and is a characteristic plant species that will catch your eye, but Apache plum, desert willow, rabbitbrush, buckwheat and juniper are also found.

The Sonoran Desert

The Sonoran Desert covers parts of California and Arizona in the U.S. and Baja California in Mexico. At 210,000 square miles, it is one of the largest deserts in North America, and with world-record high temperatures, it is also one of the hottest. To differentiate it from the Mojave, the Sonoran Desert is sometimes referred to as the Low Desert; it is also sometimes called the Gila Desert after the Gila River, or the Colorado Desert, which is the subregion of the greater Sonoran at its most northwestern extent, where it enters Southern California. The Colorado-Sonoran Desert covers 2500 square miles of land east of Los Angeles and San Diego, extending from the San Bernardino Mountains east and southeast to the Colorado River and including the Coachella and Imperial valleys and the Salton Sea (the largest lake in California). The desert is bound and crossed by several mountain ranges; it is bordered on the west by the San Jacinto and Santa Rosa mountains and on the north and east by the San Bernardino Mountains. The San Andreas Fault crosses the valley from the Chocolate Mountains in the southeast.

HUMAN-ALTERED LANDSCAPES AND URBAN ENVIRONMENTS

The impact of human activity on natural environments is visible throughout California. No brief outline of Southern California's important habitats would be complete without a mention of towns and cities, which are mostly squeezed up along the coast, making the region the most populated in all the United States.

Biodiversity is at its highest along the suburban fringe, where a botanical anarchy of remnant native plants, endemic species, hybrids, garden escapees and exotic introduced species (such as the bluegum eucalyptus from Australia that grows with zeal on roadsides and throughout much of the coastline) all compete for a foothold. The wildlife is also diverse with naturally occurring native species as well as endemic species and subspecies, hybrids of native and non-native introduced species as well as exotic pet escapees that survive the mild climate. Strategic species, whether native or introduced, take advantage of evolving opportunities for food, shelter and breeding territory. Birdfeeders, birdhouses and bat houses are established to deliberately accommodate the species we appreciate, and artificial lakes and urban parks offer additional alternatives; wharfs and ports, garbage dumps and our own homes seem to attract the species we consider to be pests. Many of the most common plants and animals in these altered landscapes were not present before the arrival of Europeans and modern transportation. In fact, California, Hawaii and Florida have the highest number of introduced species and ratio of introduced versus native species in the country. The best established of the introduced species exemplify how co-habitation with humans offers a distinct set of living situations for many plants and animals.

THE SEASONS

California's climate and seasons influence plants and animals. Aside from airborne creatures such as bats and birds, or marine species such as whales and fish, most species are confined to relatively slow forms of terrestrial travel. As a result, they have limited geographic ranges and must cope in various ways with the changing seasons. Precipitation (its presence, absence, seasonal abundance and form) has the most critical influence on vegetation, thereby determining the availability of food and shelter. Average annual precipitation is directly affected by landform, with coastal or windward slopes receiving the greatest share. Most of Southern California generally receives very little precipitation in summer, and what little the area does receive is often the result of an active fog belt along the coast.

To the west of the mountain ranges, Southern California has a Mediterranean climate, one of only five such climates in the world not adjacent to the Mediterranean Sea; to the east of the mountains are the deserts. The California Mediterranean division is on the Pacific Coast between latitudes 30° and 45° N. The climate is characterized and defined as a transition zone between the wet, cool Pacific Coast and the dry west coast desert, creating alternate wet and dry seasons. Summer droughts last for two to four rainless months and are combined with heat that causes severe evaporation. Plants have to be specifically adapted to this harsh climate. A hot, dry summer and cool, wet winter is a unique combination of seasons that creates a climate type suitable for sclerophyll forests, woodlands and scrub with hard-leaved evergreen plants.

The Transverse and Peninsular ranges have hot, dry summers and mild, rainy winters; annual average temperatures range from 32° to 60° F. Precipitation ranges from 12 to 40 inches per year, with drought in summer and what little moisture there is coming mainly from fog; fires in the chaparral and shrub areas are commonly set by lightning (or by human carelessness). In winter, there is rain but very little snow, and what falls melts quickly.

Temperatures in the Sierran climate range from 35° to 52° F but because of the elevation difference throughout this region (elevations range from 2000 to 8000 feet; some peaks reach 12,000 feet), the season can be very different from one place to the next. At high elevations, winters tend to be snowy and cold, whereas in areas of low elevation, winters are rainy and cool. Summers everywhere tend to be quite dry, but high elevations are still only cool to warm. The western slopes get significantly more precipitation with moisture from the coast, whereas the eastern slopes are in the rain shadow.

In the coastal sage scrub, the climate is always mild. Winter temperatures rarely drop to freezing, and summers occasionally reach 100° F, with fog and overcast days common. In the chaparral, the winters are also mild, only rarely enduring a hard freeze, but high summer temperatures are more common as this zone climbs out from under the marine layer. The coastal region is milder than the interior and receives some moisture in summer from the marine layer of fog; annual precipitation along the coast and into the chaparral is 12 to 35 inches.

Woodland communities, such as the foothill, Joshua tree and pinyon-juniper woodlands, endure hot, dry summers, but the winters cool off to about 10° F and can drop to freezing in the foothill woodlands. Even though the days are hot, nights in the Joshua tree woodlands and the desert are cool. In winter, evening temperatures can drop to near freezing and snow flurries can occur, even in midday; once the sun returns, however, the snow quickly melts away. The Joshua tree woodland only receives 5 to 10 inches of precipitation per year. The foothill woodlands have a higher average precipitation of 15 to 35 inches, whereas the pinyon-juniper woodlands receive 7 to 20 inches per year, and evapotranspiration may be four times greater than annual precipitation. Creosote b ush scrub receives only 5 to 10 inches of precipitation per year, and winter temperatures may briefly drop below freezing.

The deserts are hot and dry; the highest temperature ever recorded in the U.S. was 134° F in 1913 at Death Valley (a record topped only by the Sahara Desert by 2° F in 1922); however, the average annual temperature ranges from 60° to 70° F because of the moderate winters and even occasional frosts. Gentle rains occur in winter, but rain is almost unheard of in summer—the annual precipitation ranges from 2 to 10 inches in the valleys and up to 25 inches on mountain slopes, but evaporation rates in summer are very high.

Summers may be a time of growth and recovery from winter, or a time of stress from heat and aridity. An important aspect of seasonality is its effect on species composition. Some migratory species head south for warmer climes, and some enter our area from the even colder Arctic. A few alpine areas in Southern California have a true winter, with sparse food availability, temperatures below freezing and significant snowfall; here some animals that do not migrate must eat vast quantities of food in summer to build up fat reserves, others work furiously to stockpile food caches in safe places, and yet others reach the end of their life cycles come winter, leaving spring for the next generation. Some mountain species, such as ground squirrels and American black bears, may be dormant in winter. Conversely, many ungulates may be more visible in winter, when they enter lowland meadows to find edible vegetation. For some of the more charismatic species, fall is the time for mating. At this time of year, male bighorn sheep demonstrate extremes of aggression and vigilance. Many small mammals, however, such as voles and mice, mate every few months or even year-round. Along the mild coastline and foothills, species do not hibernate because there is no harsh winter to escape. Desert plants may be dormant in summer and in full bloom in winter; desert animals may also be inactive by day or even stay in their burrows for days on end, slowing their metabolisms to survive the heat and becoming more active in winter.

Whether you visit the mountains, the coast or the deserts of Southern California, you will observe different species in summer than in winter.

PROTECTED AREAS WITHIN SOUTHERN CALIFORNIA

Channel Islands National Park

Five of the eight islands, which are the tips of the spines of the seaward extension of the Santa Monica Mountains, their surrounding one nautical mile of ocean and 125,000 acres of submerged land comprise Channel Islands National Park. On a clear day some of the islands can be seen from the mainland. Santa Cruz, Santa Rosa, Santa Barbara, San Miguel and Anacapa, the most northerly of the eight islands, were granted national park status by Congress in 1980, in recognition of their unique natural and cultural resources. Island endemism is high and human impact is relatively low, making these islands a biodiversity hotspot.

Joshua Tree National Park

This protected area was designated Joshua Tree National Monument in 1936 by Franklin D. Roosevelt upon the insistence of botanist and activist Minerva Hoyt, who saw the need to protect this rare ecosystem. It was then identified as a national wilderness by congress in 1976. Joshua Tree National Park was finally established in 1994. Botanically unique, in part owing to the magnificent and numerous Joshua trees themselves, the area is also geologically fascinating with a landscape fashioned by active faults, alluvial fans and bajadas. Joshua trees are found throughout the Mojave Desert but nowhere else on Earth; Joshua Tree National Park protects one of the largest groves of this rare tree. Many species of desert plants and several palm tree oases support an abundance of life—including many rare, endemic and endangered wildlife species—in this extreme climate. The park is part of the Mojave and Colorado Deserts Biosphere Reserve, recognized by the United Nations, and has a great range of desert biodiversity.

Death Valley National Park

Despite its foreboding name, Death Valley can be an exciting place for a holiday. The national park covers more than 3.3 million acres of western Mojave Desert (making it the largest national park in the contiguous United States), and elevations range from 282 feet below sea level at the Badwater Basin saltpan (the lowest point in North America) to 11,049 feet at the summit of Telescope Peak. This park includes many extreme zones such as saltpans, subalpine and even some regions that rank among the hottest and driest places on earth. All plant and animal species found here exhibit adaptations to help them survive in extreme conditions.

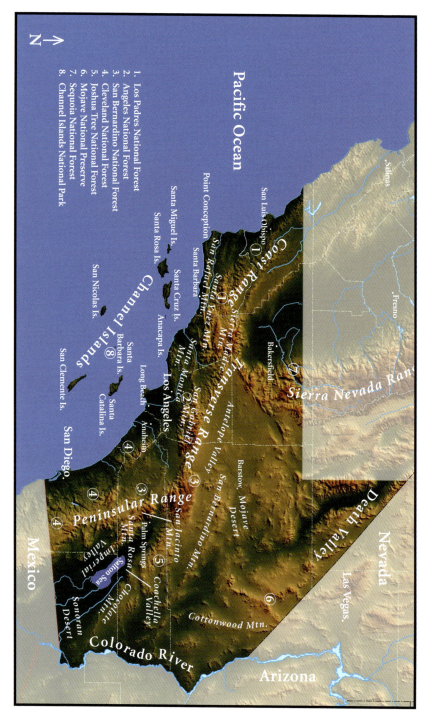

1. Los Padres National Forest
2. Angeles National Forest
3. San Bernardino National Forest
4. Cleveland National Forest
5. Joshua Tree National Park
6. Mojave National Preserve
7. Sequoia National Forest
8. Channel Islands National Park

N →

Pacific Ocean

Salinas

Fresno

San Luis Obispo

Point Conception

Santa Barbara

Coast Range

Santa Maria

San Rafael Mtns.

Sierra Madre Mtns.

Santa Ynez Mtns.

Bakersfield

Sierra Nevada Range

Santa Miguel Is.

Santa Rosa Is.

Santa Cruz Is.

Channel Islands (8)

Anacapa Is.

San Nicolas Is.

Santa Monica Mtn.

San Gabriel Mtn.

Los Angeles

Transverse Range

Antelope Valley

Barstow

Death Valley

Nevada

Las Vegas

Long Beach

Santa Barbara Is.

Santa Catalina Is.

Anaheim

San Clemente Is.

San Diego

Mexico

Peninsular Range

Salton Sea

Imperial Valley

Chocolate Mtn.

Sonoran Desert

Colorado River

Arizona

Santa Rosa Mtn.

Palm Springs

San Jacinto Mtn.

Coachella Valley

San Bernardino Mtn.

Mojave Desert

Cottonwood Mtn.

Santa Monica Mountains National Recreation Area

The Santa Monica Mountains provide a backdrop for the city of Los Angeles and stretch northward along the coastline of the Santa Monica Bay, creating coastal cliffs and rocky shores. They were formed from the collision of the plates along the San Andreas Fault, which is responsible for California's infamous earthquakes. In 1976, Congress designated this national recreation area as a part of the national park system. The coastal mountain environment offers a mild climate for hundreds of species of birds and more than 50 species of mammals, including deer, mountain lions and coyotes.

Mojave National Preserve

The Kelso Dunes, the volcanic formations such as the sculpted sandstone at Hole-in-the-Wall and the cinder cone lava beds, and one of the oldest groves of Joshua trees are just a few of the reasons this impressive work of nature was designated a national preserve in October 1994. Located between Los Angeles and Las Vegas, Nevada, Mojave National Preserve is a recommended retreat into nature from either of these urban jungles.

Sequoia National Forest and Giant Sequoia National Monument

In April 2000, former President Bill Clinton proclaimed the establishment of Giant Sequoia National Monument while standing alongside one of the great trees of the Trail of 100 Giants. There are approximately 125 giant sequoias with base diameters greater than 10 feet in this grove of more than 700 mature individuals of this incredible tree. Sequoia National Forest comprises 341 acres and protects this grove, in which the oldest individuals are estimated to be 1500 years old.

Los Padres National Forest

Extending over several counties, stretching over 220 miles from north to south, and composed of approximately 1.75 million acres of the Coast and Transverse ranges, this enormous greenbelt provides a range of forest habitat from coastal to montane to semi-desert and is a refuge for hundreds of species of wildlife. The forest in its entirety consists of two separate divisions: one in the north in Monterey County, the other in Southern California including lands in the counties of San Luis Obispo, Santa Barbara, Ventura and Los Angeles. Within the forest there are two California condor sanctuaries, the Sisquoc in Santa Barbara and the Sespe in Ventura.

Angeles National Forest

About one hour's drive (traffic depending!) from the megalopolis of Los Angeles is this 655,387-acre forest. The forest is located in the San Gabriel Mountains, whose highest peak is Mount San Antonio (also known as Mount Baldy), at 10,064 feet. The park hosts a section of the Pacific Crest Trail (a hiking and equestrian trail that runs from the border of Mexico to the border of Canada following the coastal crest of the Sierra Nevada and Cascade ranges). This national forest is now more than a century old.

San Bernardino National Forest

Two divisions of this forest total over 800,000 acres of wilderness area along the San Bernardino Mountains (the eastern section of the Transverse Range) and the San Jacinto and Santa Rosa mountains (the northern reaches of the Peninsular Range). The western border of this forest joins Angeles National Forest, to which it was once combined. There are hundreds of miles of trails and an impressive diversity of both desert and montane species. Big Bear Lake is one of the most popular recreation areas for Los Angelinos who want to cool off during the hot, dry summer.

Cleveland National Forest

The southernmost national forest in California is the outdoor recreation getaway for San Diego residents. It is composed of 460,000 acres of chaparral and riparian habitat. The Cedar Fire, the largest wildfire in California history, burnt its way through Cleveland National Forest in October 2003, consuming 280,278 acres, destroying habitat and homes and taking human life. The Santa Ana Mountains rise within this threatened forest wilderness, which is completely surrounded by urban development; conservationists are working to protect the area's diversity, which includes a grove of century-old Jeffrey pine and several endangered animal species.

California Poppy Reserve

This area in Antelope Valley (along with Arthur B. Ripley Desert State Park—also located in the valley—which preserves a stand of Joshua trees and junipers is the place to be when the poppies are in spring bloom and are blanketing the area with color.

There are dozens of state parks, big and small, in Southern California—some preserving the last of a rare ecosystem or species, others protecting vast areas with foresight and appreciation, and all well worth visiting.

OBSERVING NATURE

Many types of wildlife are most active at night, especially in the desert, so the best times for viewing are during the "wildlife hours" at dawn and dusk. At these times of day, animals are out of their daytime hideouts or roosting sites and more easily encountered. During winter in the mountains, hunger may force certain mammals to be more active during midday when temperatures are warmest; conversely, midday is when some animals may become less active and less visible in the hot summer. Within the protected reserves and national parks of California, many of the larger mammals can be viewed easily from the safety of a vehicle; if you walk backcountry trails, however, you are typically within the territory of certain mammals with which close encounters are best avoided.

Whale watching can either be an organized activity with tourist boats taking groups of enthusiasts out to known areas of high whale and dolphin sightings, or it can be a random moment of fortune right from the shore as many species frequent inshore waters.

Although whale watching has strong merit in educating the public and increasing awareness and appreciation for marine mammals and the health of the oceans, it can be disruptive to cetacean behavior, and tour groups must be considerate and passive in the presence of these sensitive species. A good time of year for seeing whales in Southern California is between January and March, when gray whales pass by on their migration from their Arctic feeding grounds to the warm breeding grounds in Baja California. Between June and October, blue and humpback whales are more frequently seen passing along our shores.

Birdwatching is becoming an increasingly popular activity for many people, from serious "birders" to those who simply wish to recognize and appreciate the diversity of attractive, interesting birds. There are scores of excellent books, on-line resources, clubs and organizations to learn from. When practiced with patience and reserve, birdwatching is a low-impact pastime and a ready source of mental and physical exercise: with perhaps hundreds of resident and migratory species, Southern California offers endless exploration and satisfaction for birders. This nature guide presents only a brief overview, but there are hundreds of bird species to discover in Southern California. One does not have to go far to see birds either; the 600-acre Ballona Wetlands in Playa del Rey, for example, have an amazing diversity of birdlife to observe adjacent to the beach and marina of Marina del Rey, south of Venice Beach in Los Angeles. One must be patient, though, because birds are among the most highly mobile animals; they may be seen clearly and closely one moment and then become little more than a backlit, rapidly vanishing speck in the next!

Although people have become more con-scious of the need to respect and protect wild-life and wild spaces, the pressures of increased human visitation can have a negative impact, so we must raise public awareness not only to appreciate nature but to do so while employing courtesy and com-mon sense. Honor both the encounter and the animal by demonstrating a respect appropriate to the occasion. Here are some points to remember for ethical wildlife watching:

- Stress is harmful to wildlife, so never chase or flush animals from cover or try to catch or touch them. Use binoculars and keep a respectful distance, for the animal's sake and often for your own.

- Leave the environment, including both flora and fauna, unchanged by your visits. Tread lightly and take home only pictures and memories. Do not pick wildflowers, and do not collect sea stars, sea urchins or seashells still occu-pied by the sea animal. Amphibians are especially sensitive to being touched or held, especially if you have sunscreen or insect repellant on your skin, which can poison the animal.

- Pets are a hindrance to wildlife viewing. They may chase, injure or kill other animals, so control your pets or leave them at home.

- Do not litter, and litter includes cigarette butts. Dropping butts on the ground is not only disrespectful to the environment and other people try-ing to enjoy a natural area, it is also potentially dangerous, because in Cali-fornia the risk of accidentally starting a wildfire is high. Carry your butts in a pocket or bag until you can dis-pose of them responsibly.

- Take the time to learn about wildlife and the behavior and sensitivity of each species.

ANIMALS

A nimals are mammals, birds, reptiles, amphibians, fish and invertebrates, all of which belong to the Kingdom Animalia. They obtain energy by ingesting food that they hunt or gather. Mammals and birds are endothermic, meaning their body temperature is internally regulated and will stay nearly constant despite the surrounding environmental temperature unless that temperature is extreme and persistent. Reptiles, amphibians, fish and invertebrates are ectothermic, meaning that they do not have the ability to regulate their own internal body temperature and tend to be the same temperature as their surroundings. Animals reproduce sexually, and they have a limited growth that is reached at sexual maturity. They also have diverse and complicated behaviors displayed in courtship, defense, parenting, playing, fighting, eating, hunting, in their social hierarchy, and in how they deal with environmental stresses such as weather, change of season or availability of food and water.

MAMMALS

Mammals are the group to which human beings belong. The general characteristics of a mammal include being endothermic, bearing live young (with the exception of echidnas and the platypus), nursing their young and having hair or fur on their bodies. In general, all mammals larger than rodents are sexually dimorphic, meaning that the male and the female are different in appearance by size or other diagnostics, such as antlers. Males are usually larger than females. The different groups of mammals are herbivores, carnivores, omnivores or insectivores. People often associate large mammals with wilderness, making these animals prominent symbols in Native legends and stirring emotional connections with people in modern times.

Hoofed Mammals
pp. 48–51

Bears
p. 51

Cats
p. 52

Dogs
pp. 53–54

Whales & Dolphins
pp. 55–59

Seals & Sea-lions
pp. 60–61

Otters
p. 61

Weasels & Skunks
pp. 62–63

Raccoons
p. 64

Porcupine
p. 65

Beavers
pp. 65–66

Mice & Kin
pp. 66–68

Squirrels
pp. 69–70

Hares & Rabbits
pp. 70–71

Bats
pp. 71–74

Moles & Shrews
pp. 74–75

Opossum
p. 75

American Bison

Bison bison

Length: 6½–13 ft (tail 12–28 in)
Shoulder height: 3½–6½ ft
Weight: 790–2400 lb

Bison amongst the palm-treed Southern Californian backdrop is indeed an odd juxtaposition, but reintroduced populations are protected on the equally rare grasslands in the southern part of the state. Bison never existed in large numbers in California, but they did range here in the historic era when their North American numbers were in the millions. • Both sexes have short, round, upward curving, black horns atop their massive woolly heads. The head, high shoulder hump and forequarters are covered with shaggy fur. **Where found:** select private and public ranches, protected areas; reintroduced population on Catalina Island and around Camp Pendelton in San Diego County. **Also known as:** American buffalo.

Bighorn Sheep

Ovis canadensis

Length: 5–6 ft (tail 3–5 in)
Shoulder height: 30–45 in
Weight: 120–340 lb

Icons of North American wilderness, male bighorn sheep are well known for their spectacular head-butting clashes during the fall rut. Both sexes have brown horns, but males' are thick and curved forward. • Bighorn sheep are native to mountainous regions of California; mountain meadows provide bighorns with feeding grounds, and rocky outcroppings provide protection from predators, namely eagles, mountain lions and bobcats, which prey on the lambs. **Where found:** typically on rugged mountain slopes, cliffs and alpine meadows; some populations in rolling foothills or beyond the mountains in arid badland regions if precipitous slopes, food and water are present; southeastern parts of the state. **Also known as:** mountain sheep.

Elk

Cervus elaphus

Length: 6–9 ft (tail 4½–7 in)
Shoulder height: 4–5 ft
Weight: 400–1000 lb

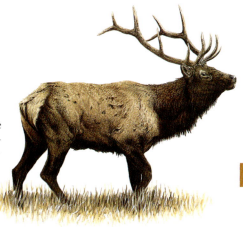

The haunting, high-pitched bugle calls of rutting male elk are a hallmark of fall. A male's large, spreading antlers may span 5 ft and weigh up to 30 lb. During the fall rut and in spring when females are with calves, elk can be very dangerous and should be avoided. • Elk tend to be shy forest dwellers, moving to open meadows at dusk to feed until dawn. • There are 2 subspecies of elk in Southern California: Rocky Mountain (*C. e. nelsoni*) and tule (*C. e. nannodes*), differentiated by slight variances in color and size. **Where found:** mixed forests, coniferous forests, mountain meadows and lake shorelines up to the treeline; Rocky Mountain elk have been introduced into Kern and San Luis Obispo counties; tule elk are found in scattered populations in the south-central counties. **Also known as:** wapiti.

Mule Deer

Odocoileus hemionus

Length: 4–6 ft (tail 4½–9 in)
Shoulder height: 3–3½ ft
Weight: 68–470 lb

Mule deer form large bands, particularly in winter. They prefer hilly terrain, where they use bounding hops, like those of jackrabbits, called "stotting" or "pronking" to escape predators. • These deer are named for their very large, mule-like ears. Large ears and a black-tipped tail are the best field marks for this ungulate. • Bucks in the fall rut compete for females by tangling antlers and forcing the opponent's head down, reminiscent of arm wrestling. **Where found:** widespread; dry brushlands, meadows, open woodlands, riparian areas in dry arid regions; in summer and fall, bucks tend to remain at higher elevations while does and fawns stay at lower elevations; in winter all move to low valleys and meadows; throughout the Sierra Nevada Range, west of the Transverse Range, throughout most of the south of the state and on the Channel Islands. **Also known as:** black-tailed deer.

Pronghorn

Antilocapra americana

Length: 4–5 ft (tail 3½–6 in)
Shoulder height: 32–41 in
Weight: 70–140 lb

Often incorrectly referred to as an antelope, the pronghorn is actually the sole member of the family Antilocapridae (true antelopes belong to the Bovidae family along with cows, goats and sheep). The males' branched horns are shed like antlers (some females have short unbranched horns). • The pronghorn is the fastest animal in the Western Hemisphere, able to retain continuous 20-ft bounds at up to 60 mph, yet it cannot jump a fence. Fences in managed pronghorn territory are higher so the animals can duck underneath, which they can do at a full run without breaking stride. **Where found:** open grasslands, sagebrush plains, alkali deserts and riparian and scrub habitats; since 1982, small populations from Northern California reintroduced to Kern, San Luis Obispo and San Benito counties.

Feral Horse

Equus caballus

Length: up to 7 ft (tail up to 3 ft)
Shoulder height: 3½–5½ ft
Weight: 590–860 lb

Although the domesticated horse is common across North America, wild horses spark the romantic imagination of many people who see this introduced species as a symbol of freedom and a vestige of what remains wild in the West. Feral horses are descendants of domestic horses but have run wild for hundreds of years, from the Rocky Mountains to the Southwest. • Wild horses are distinguishable from domestic horses by their long manes and tails and by their pronounced behavioral patterns between members of the herd. • A population of feral horses, known as Picacho wild horses, can be found in the southern foothills of the Chocolate Mountains (the Little Picacho Wilderness). Wild burros also live in the area. **Where found:** small populations occur along the southeast portion of the state. **Also known as:** mustang.

Feral Pig

Sus scrofa

Length: 4½–6 ft (tail up to 12 in)
Shoulder height: 21–43 in
Weight: *Male:* 165–440 lb; *Female:* 77–330 lb

One typically thinks of a chubby, pink, bald, docile animal when envisioning a pig. Domestic pigs were bred to lose many of their wild features, which include a coarse, dense fur coat, long, straight, sparsely furred tail and tusks (or modified canines). However, that domestic pig is the same species as its wild relative that was introduced to North America from Europe and Asia. The wild pig is not docile in its demeanor—it is dangerously aggressive. • Wild and domestic pigs have hybridized in California, although "purebred" feral pigs still exist. **Where found:** forested mountain and brushy areas, wetlands, ravines and ridges in parks and preserves; along the central coast as far south as Santa Barbara. **Also known as:** wild boar, wild pig, wild hog.

American Black Bear

Ursus americanus

Length: 4½–6 ft (tail 3–7 in)
Shoulder height: 3–4 ft
Weight: 88–595 lb

The black bear's pelage is most commonly black but varies to cinnamon brown and to honey blond, with a lighter-colored muzzle. This omnivore eats plant material and obtains protein from insects such as bees (often while on honey raids), scavenged meat or, rarely, hunting small mammals. The black bear spends winter in a den, but the hibernation is not deep, and the bear may rouse from its torpor and exit the den on mild winter days. • Although emblematic and on the state flag, the grizzly bear (*U. arctos horribilis*) is extirpated from California; the last one was shot in 1922, but the species became the state mammal nonetheless in 1953. **Where found:** in most forested regions throughout Southern California.

Mountain Lion

Felis concolor

Length: 5–9 ft (tail 25–32 in)
Shoulder height: 26–32 in
Weight: 70–190 lb

The powerful, majestic mountain lion is a large, secretive cat. It is seldom seen by people, but studies over the past 30 years estimate the population by studying densities within different habitat types around the state, which vary from zero to 10 lions per 100 mi². Expanding the densities over the total amount of each habitat type available provides a crude estimate of 4000–6000 mountain lions statewide. • More than half of California is prime habitat for this cat, which is found wherever mule deer are present. Mountain lions often hunt by sitting in trees above animal trails waiting to pounce on prey. **Where found:** foothills and mountains from low-elevation valleys to treeline, riparian habitats and brushlands; in small numbers throughout much of Southern California where suitable habitat exists. **Also known as:** cougar, puma.

Bobcat

Lynx rufus

Length: 2½–4 ft (tail 5–7 in)
Shoulder height: 17–20 in
Weight: 15–29 lb

The nocturnal bobcat feeds on a wide range of prey, including rabbits, voles, mice, birds, reptiles and insects. Small but mighty, the bobcat is even capable of bringing down a deer by the throat if the opportunity presents itself. • This cat's atypically short "bobbed" tail is well suited to the shrubby and forested areas in which it hunts, but the bobcat is highly adaptable and may even be seen close to residential areas. • Like most young cats, bobcat kittens are almost always at play. **Where found:** in coniferous and deciduous forests, brushy areas, riparian habitats and all parts of chaparral country; throughout Southern California.

Coyote

Canis latrans

Length: 3½–4½ ft (tail 12–16 in)
Shoulder height: 23–26 in
Weight: 18–44 lb

Coyotes occasionally form loose packs and join in spirited yipping choruses. These intelligent and versatile hunter-scavengers are best described as opportunistic omnivores. They have been observed fishing or even engaging the help of a hunting badger to catch ground squirrels. • Once extirpated from California, along with the wolf, the coyote has made a comeback, and because of its adaptable and cunning behavior, it has thrived. **Where found:** mixed and coniferous forests, meadows, agricultural lands and suburban areas; almost every valley and most cities throughout Southern California host a population.

Gray Fox

Urocyon cinereoargenteus

Length: 30–43 in (tail 11–17 in)
Shoulder height: 14–15 in
Weight: 7½–13 lb

Preferring rocky, shrub-covered and forested terrain and avoiding populated areas, the mainly nocturnal gray fox is the most common fox in California, yet it is seldom seen unless you know where to look for it. • Most remarkable is this fox's ability to climb trees—the only member of the dog family able to do so—to escape danger, pursue birds or find egg-filled nests. It may even use a high tree-hollow for a den. • The gray fox's fur is shorter and denser than that of the red fox. **Where found:** open forests, woodlands, shrublands and rocky areas throughout Southern California; a similar but smaller (about the size of a house cat) species *(U. littoralis)* called the island fox inhabits the Channel Islands and is a federally protected endangered species.

Kit Fox

Vulpes macrotis

Length: 24–33 in
(tail 9–13 in)
Shoulder height: 12 in
Weight: 3–6 lb

This nocturnal fox is also shy and secretive, making it a rare sight for lucky wildlife enthusiasts. Most people must make do with seeing this fox's tracks in the desert sands of its arid habitat. • Kit foxes suffer depredation from coyotes and compete for habitat and prey with bobcats and other species of fox. • Some academics believe the kit fox is a subspecies of the swift fox (*V. velox*). Molecular genetic analysis suggests the two are distinct species but it is still inconclusive; however, they interbreed where their ranges overlap in New Mexico and Texas. • Three populations of kit fox are recognized in California: the endangered San Joaquin population, the desert kit fox of the Mojave Desert and the now extinct southern California kit fox of the southern desert regions of the state. **Where found:** the Mohave Desert and sagebrush and grassland habitats of southeastern California.

Red Fox

Vulpes vulpes

Length: 3–3½ ft (tail 14–17 in)
Shoulder height: 15 in
Weight: 8–15 lb

The red fox is a talented mouser with high-pouncing antics that are much more cat-like than dog-like. The entertaining, extroverted behavior and noble good looks of the red fox have landed it roles in many fairy tales, fables and Native legends. • The red fox is typically a vivid reddish orange, but its coat has darker color phases with dark fur across the back and shoulders, or it can be almost entirely black with silver-tipped hairs. The tip of its elegant, bushy tail, however, is always white. **Where found:** grasslands, coastal scrub, chaparral, chamise, riparian and wetland areas and forest edges (avoiding dense forests); in Ventura, Los Angeles and Orange counties.

Gray Whale

Eschrichtius robustus

Length: average 45 ft; up to 50 ft
Weight: average 35 tons; up to 45 tons

The sole member of the gray whale family, this baleen whale lacks the significant throat pleating of the rorqual whales. Its gray skin is covered with a speckling of barnacles and carries large communities of other organisms, such as whale lice, along for the ride. • The gray whale is famous for its lengthy migrations that take it 10,000 mi from the arctic seas in summer to the Mexican coast in winter, thrilling whale watchers along the entire Pacific Coast as it passes by. **Where found:** during winter migration, inshore and offshore all along the coast of Southern California. **Also known as:** devilfish, mussel-digger, scrag whale.

Minke Whale

Balaenoptera acutorostrata

Length: average 27 ft; up to 35 ft
Weight: average 10 tons; up to 15 tons

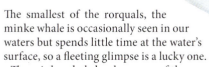

The smallest of the rorquals, the minke whale is occasionally seen in our waters but spends little time at the water's surface, so a fleeting glimpse is a lucky one. • The minke whale has been one of the more heavily hunted of the baleen whales since the 1980s, when larger whale populations had already collapsed. **Where found:** offshore all along the coast of Southern California; migrates seasonally between warm and cold waters. **Also known as:** piked whale, sharp-headed finner, little finner, lesser finback, lesser rorqual.

Fin Whale

Balaenoptera physalus

Length: average 70 ft; up to 89 ft
Weight: average 80 tons; up to 140 tons

When this long, sleek giant swims leisurely and gracefully along the surface of the water, its tall, narrow, dense blow reaches up to 20 ft high and is very noticeable on the horizon, but the whale does not show its fluke when beginning a dive. • The fin whale can be found singly or in pairs but is more often in pods of 3–7 individuals. On occasion, several pods have been observed in a small area, creating concentrations of as many as 50 animals. • Fin whales are exceptionally fast movers and have been clocked at 20 mph in short bursts. **Where found:** offshore all along the coast of Southern California.

Humpback Whale

Megaptera novaeangliae

Length: average 45 ft; up to 62 ft
Weight: average 30 tons; up to 53 tons

The haunting songs of humpbacks can last from a few minutes to a few hours or can even be epic, days-long concerts; they have inspired both scientists and artists and can reach out to the imaginations of many people who listen and wonder what these great creatures are saying. • These rorquals—baleen whales with throats of pleated, expandable skin—employ a unique hunting strategy. They make a bubble net to round their prey into a tight cluster, thereby obtaining a food-dense gulp. **Where found:** offshore in summer along the coast of Southern California; migrates in winter to the waters off Mexico or Costa Rica, or to Hawaii to mate and calve.

Blue Whale

Balaenoptera musculus

Length: average 85 ft; up to 110 ft
Weight: average 120 tons; up to 200 tons

This, the largest whale, largest mammal and largest animal on the planet, has a very tongue-in-cheek scientific species name, *musculus*, which translates from Latin as "little mouse." This highly endangered species is sometimes seen off the coast of California; its total population has been recovering from intense whaling since the International Whaling Commission gave it protected status in 1966. **Where found:** feeding near the coast in summer and fall, most commonly around Point Conception; migrates south in winter.

Orca

Orcinus orca

Length: average 28 ft; up to 32 ft
Weight: average 7½ tons; up to 11 tons

Few people would not recognize this iconic creature, which is found around the world. It is revered in legend and as a totem by Native Americans, celebrated by enthusiastic whale watchers and, unfortunately, cheered on for entertainment in captivity. • Researchers have identified 3 distinct types of killer whale along the Pacific Coast: transients, residents and offshore types. Transients and residents differ in many ways, including home range size, morphology, hunting preferences and social behavior; offshore types are similar to residents but range farther from the coast. Residents are uncommon in Southern California; the offshore and transient types are more commonly observed. **Where found:** offshore or in cooler coastal waters all along the coast of Southern California. **Also known as:** killer whale.

Bottlenose Dolphin

Tursiops truncatus

Length: average 10 ft; up to 13 ft
Weight: average 440 lb; up to 1430 lb

Most familiar to the public through aquariums, TV shows and various celebrity endorsements, the bottlenose dolphin is one of the cetaceans most highly studied by marine biologists and behavioral ecologists. Social, behavioral and physical differences between inshore and offshore populations are being studied; in California, local conservation organizations have been photo-identifying the inshore bottlenose dolphin population, which is now estimated to be around 450 individuals. • Markings on the skin and dorsal fins are as distinctive and personal as a fingerprint. **Where found:** regularly observed in inshore and offshore waters all along the coast of Southern California.

Short-beaked Common Dolphin

Delphinus delphis

Length: average 6½ ft; up to 8½ ft
Weight: average 170 lb; up to 300 lb

Brilliant acrobatics accompany the thrill of having a group of common dolphins swim alongside your boat. They love to bow-ride (riding the momentum of the current made under the bow of a swift-moving boat) and can occur in very large groups of 50–1000 individuals. • The long-beaked common dolphin (*D. capensis*) is very similar both physically and behaviorally to the short-beaked, but a trained eye can observe the characteristic distinctions. **Where found:** regularly observed offshore all along the coast of Southern California.

Risso's Dolphin

Grampus griseus

Length: average 10 ft; up to 13 ft
Weight: average 880 lb;
up to 1100 lb

Risso's dolphins have an interesting social behavior of scratching and biting at each other, leaving white scars all over their bodies—old individuals become so scarred that they appear almost completely white. They can also become scarred from being stung by large squid, their preferred prey. • Off our shores, they are typically observed as solitary individuals or in pairs, but they can occur in large herds, from 25 to several hundred animals. • These dolphins can become quite engaged in play sessions of breaching, spy-hopping, lob-tailing and flipper and fluke slapping. **Where found:** deep, offshore waters all along the coast of Southern California.

Pacific White-sided Dolphin

Lagenorhynchus obliquidens

Length: average 6½ ft; up to 8 ft
Weight: average 220 lb; up to 300 lb

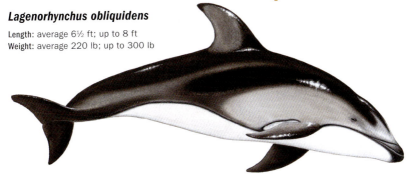

Whale watchers lucky enough to see Pacific white-sided dolphins often get some additional bonus entertainment from these highly acrobatic animals: breaching, somersaulting and bow-riding, the dolphins are seemingly very excited at the opportunity to show off. • Dolphins can focus their vision above and below water and often take a closer look at people by jumping alongside the boat or lifting their heads above the water's surface. **Where found:** open ocean; most often seen in coastal and sheltered waters, especially on the inside straits between islands and the mainland. **Also known as:** lag, Pacific striped dolphin, white-striped dolphin, hook-finned dolphin.

Northern Elephant Seal

Mirounga angustirostris

Length: *Male:* 12–16 ft; *Female:* 7–12 ft
Weight: *Male:* up to 5070 lb; *Female:* 2000 lb

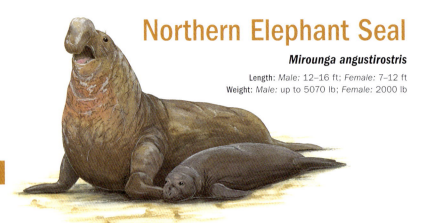

The northern elephant seal is the show-off of the seal family; it is the largest seal in the Northern Hemisphere, it dives the deepest (up to 5000 ft) and it migrates the farthest (up to 13,000 mi). Rarely seen south of Point Conception, this seal is seen around the Channel Islands in breeding season. Both sexes sport the large snout, but that of the adult male is a pendulous, inflatable (for producing impressive rattling snorts), foot-long "trunk" analogous to that of its common namesake. **Where found:** northern Channel Islands or swimming offshore; Point Conception is considered the limit of its southern range.

Harbor Seal

Phoca vitulina

Length: 4–6 ft (tail 3½–4½ in)
Weight: 110–310 lb

Year-round, great colonies of harbor seals can be observed either basking in the day or sleeping at night on rocky shores and islands. During the day, individuals can often be seen bobbing vertically in the water—the harbor seal cannot sleep at the surface in the manner in which sea otters can, but it can actually sleep underwater, going without breathing for up to 20 minutes. • These seals are shy of humans but do occasionally pop their heads up beside a canoe or kayak to investigate, then make a quick retreat. **Where found:** bays and estuaries, intertidal sandbars and rocky shorelines all along the coast of Southern California.

California Sea-lion

Zalophus californianus

Length: *Male:* 6½–8 ft; *Female:* 4½–6½ ft
Weight: *Male:* 440–860 lb; *Female:* 100–250 lb

If you spend any time on the water off the
coast of California, you are likely
to encounter California sea-
lions. They lounge about
on large buoys, fre-
quent marinas, pop
up alongside canoe-
ists and kayakers
and swim up to
divers and surfers.
California sea-lions
are non-aggressive, often
playful and quite intelligent,
as shown by their ability to learn
and perform an array of tricks and stunts in captivity. • Female California sea-lions
can be seen year-round in Southern California, whereas the males are typically
only this far south in their range during the spring breeding season (May/June);
breeding rookeries are found on the Channel Islands. **Where found:** in coastal
waters, around islands and on rocky or sandy beaches and floating offshore buoys
all along the coast of Southern California.

Sea Otter

Enhydra lutris

Length: 2½–5½ ft (tail 10–16 in)
Weight: 50–100 lb

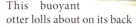

This   buoyant
otter lolls about on its back
like a sunbather, floating in a manner
us humans can only somewhat achieve in the saltiest of seas. It can even sleep on
the water after anchoring itself in kelp beds, which are habitat for sea urchins, this
otter's favorite prey. Reluctant to abandon the comfortable recline, the sea otter
grooms itself and dines while floating on its back, using tools such as rocks to
crack open the shells of its prey. During its lifetime of up to 20 years, a sea otter
is rarely on land. **Where found:** almost always in the water; shallow, coastal areas
with abundant kelp beds; scattered populations along the coast, notably San Nicolas
Island (the Channel Islands) and around Point Conception.

American Marten

Martes americana

Length: 20–26 in (tail 7–9 in)
Weight: 1–3 lb

An expert climber with semi-retractable claws, this forest dweller is quick and agile enough to catch arboreal squirrels, such as the red squirrel. Although it spends most of its time on the ground, the marten often dens in a tree-hollow, where it raises its annual litter of 1–5 kits. • Most people only see a marten in the form of a fur stole—the animal is very elusive but not wary enough of the trapline, an ongoing threat even today. To see a marten in the deep forest is to know that you are in true wilderness. **Where found:** old-growth coniferous forests of spruce and fir in Kern County. **Also known as:** American sable, pine marten.

Long-tailed Weasel

Mustela frenata

Length: 11–16½ in (tail 4½–11½ in)
Weight: 3–14 oz

Following the tracks of the long-tailed weasel on a snow-covered meadow offers good insight into the curious and energetic nature of this animal. Seemingly distracted from walking in a straight line, it continuously zigs and zags to investigate everything that catches its attention. • The long-tailed weasel feeds on small rodents, birds, insects, reptiles, amphibians and, occasionally, fruits and berries. Like other true weasels, it turns white in winter, but the tip of its tail remains black. **Where found:** agricultural areas, grassy slopes, deciduous woodlands, intermontane valleys and open forests; throughout the region, except the arid southeast of the state.

Badger

Taxidea taxus

Length: 25–35 in (tail 5–6½ in)
Weight: 11–24 lb

Equipped with huge claws and strong forelimbs, the badger is an efficient digger, able to dig out a den up to 30 ft long. Once the badger moves its home, these dens are essential in providing den sites, shelters and hibernacula for many creatures, from coyotes to black widow spiders. • The badger's powerful jaws, long teeth and aggressive defense tactics make it a formidable fighter against most predators. It preys almost exclusively upon ground squirrels and other rodents. **Where found:** low-elevation fields, meadows and grasslands, fence lines and ditches; throughout Southern California south into Mexico.

Striped Skunk

Mephitis mephitis

Length: 22–32 in (tail 8–14 in)
Weight: 4–9½ lb

Only the great horned owl, a regular predator of this small mammal, is undeterred by the odor of the striped skunk. Butylmercaptan is responsible for the stink of the skunk's musk, which is sprayed in defense. If sprayed into the eyes of the skunk's perceived attacker, it causes burning, tearing and even temporary blindness.

• When undisturbed, the striped skunk is a quiet, reclusive omnivore, feeding on insects, worms, bird eggs, reptiles and amphibians, vegetation and, rarely, small mammals and carrion. **Where found:** lower-elevation streamside woodlands, groves of hardwood trees, semi-open areas, brushy grasslands and valleys, and can occur in urban environments, where it raids gardens and garbage bins; west of the Transverse and Peninsular ranges, extending along the southern and southeastern border of the state but absent from the deserts.

Western Spotted Skunk

Spilogale gracilis

Length: 13–23 in (tail 4–8 in)
Weight: 1–2 lb

When threatened, this skunk stamps its feet or makes short lunges at its perceived attacker, which will pay the smelly price if it ignores the warning. Although this assault is no laughing matter, the posture this small mammal assumes to spray

is comical—the skunk literally performs a handstand, arches its back so that its backside and tail face forward above its head, and then walks toward its assailant while spraying. • When not performing such feats of showmanship, this nocturnal skunk feeds on insects, primarily grasshoppers and crickets, but will forage opportunistically for any food source. **Where found:** woodlands, farmlands, riparian zones, rocky areas and open grasslands or scrublands; throughout southwestern California, extending along the southeastern border of the state.

Ringtail

Bassariscus astutus

Length: 25–32 in (tail 12–17 in)
Weight: 1½–2½ lb

A member of the raccoon family, the ringtail is reminiscent of a cat, even in the way it hunts by stalking and pouncing upon its prey of small mammals, reptiles and amphibians. The ringtail's omnivorous diet also includes insects, bird eggs and nestlings, carrion and fruit. • Cacomistle, an alternate name for this animal, is derived from the language of the Mexican Nahuatl people and means "half mountain lion," furthering the cat comparisons. Its bushy, ringed tail and affinity to water reveal its kinship with the raccoon. **Where found:** close to water in rocky slopes and valleys in the foothills; throughout Southern California. **Also known as:** cacomistle, civet cat, miner's cat, ring-tailed cat.

Raccoon

Procyon lotor

Length: 26–38 in
(tail 7½–16 in)
Weight: 12–31 lb

A garbage container is no match for the raccoon's curiosity, persistence and problem-solving abilities, making your trash and the garden goldfish pond prime targets for midnight food raids in urban areas. In this animal's natural habitat of forest streams, lakes and ponds, an omnivorous diet of clams, frogs, fish, bird eggs and nestlings, berries, nuts and insects is more than ample. • Raccoons build up their fat reserves during the warm months to sustain themselves throughout winter. **Where found:** lower-elevation riparian areas, forests edges and wetlands; throughout southwestern California, extending along the southeastern border of the state.

Porcupine

Erethizon dorsatum

Length: 21–37 in (tail 5½–9 in)
Weight: 8–40 lb

A porcupine cannot throw its 30,000 or so quills but delivers them into the flesh of an attacker with a quick flick of the tail. The quills are dangerous but attractive, common in traditional Native American beadwork. • This excellent tree climber has a vegetarian diet and feeds on forbs, shrubs and the sugary cambium of trees. An insatiable craving for salt occasionally drives it to gnaw on rubber tires, wooden ax handles, hiking boots and even toilet seats! • A slow-moving, nocturnal creature, the porcupine is a common roadkill victim. **Where found:** coniferous and mixed forests and wooded riparian areas; scattered distribution throughout Southern California.

Beaver

Castor canadensis

Length: 3–4 ft (tail 11–21 in)
Weight: 35–66 lb

The loud slap of a beaver's tail on water warns of intruders. A beaver can remain under water for 15 minutes, and its tail is an extremely effective propulsion device for swimming and diving. • Beavers are skillful and unrelenting in the construction and maintenance of their dams and lodges. They use their long, continuously growing incisors to cut down trees in short order, and their strong jaws can drag a 20-lb piece of wood. **Where found:** lakes, ponds, marshes and slow-flowing rivers and streams at most elevations with ample vegetation; scattered distribution in Southern California.

Common Muskrat

Ondatra zibethicus

Length: 18–24 in (tail 7½–11 in)
Weight: 1½–3½ lb

Although they have similar habitats and behaviors, the beaver and the common muskrat are not closely related. Much like the beaver, the muskrat sports large incisors that it uses to cut through a vast array of thick vegetation, particularly cattails and bulrushes, and it makes a partially submerged den similar to that of a beaver, which provides nesting spots for many geese and ducks as well as important shelter for other rodents when the muskrat moves house. **Where found:** low-elevation sloughs, lakes, marshes and streams with plenty of cattails, rushes and open water; scattered and limited distribution in Southern California.

Desert Woodrat

Neotoma lepida

Length: 11–18 in (tail 4½–9 in)
Weight: 3–18 oz

Among the great variety of nocturnal desert rodents, the desert woodrat is one of the most dominant species. • This woodrat usually makes its home in a burrow at the base of, or within, prickly pear cacti, and is staunchly territorial of its shelter and water source, driving away other rodents. • All woodrats are infamous for collecting objects, whether natural or human-made, useful or merely decorative, to add to their large, messy nests—the decorative style of this species' nest displays twigs, cactus spines, random vegetation and even human litter. **Where found:** deserts, juniper-pinyon woodlands, sagebrush and scrub areas where *Opuntia* species are present; throughout much of Southern California. **Also known as:** packrat, trade rat.

Desert Kangaroo Rat

Dipodomys deserti

Length: 12–15 in (tail 7⅛–8½ in)
Weight: 2¾–4⅞ oz

Named for its manner of hopping on its long-footed hind legs, with its short forelegs held in front like arms, the desert kangaroo rat is a dominant desert species, highly adapted to its demanding environment. It can survive without a source of free drinking water by obtaining all its water requirements from eating seeds and leaves of desert forbs and limited green vegetation in winter and spring. • The desert kangaroo rat excavates complex subterranean burrows of intertwined passageways that lead to food or nesting chambers; although it manages to burrow in its sandy habitat, it must avoid dunes that are unstable and can shift. **Where found:** desert as well as some creosote and scrub areas; southeastern California.

Norway Rat

Rattus norvegicus

Length: 13–18 in (tail 4½–8¾ in)
Weight: 7–17 oz

Introduced to North
America in 1775, the Norway rat is so successful that it is the most common rodent to be seen. This rat owes its success to its adaptive, tolerant nature, which allows it to exploit any available food source or shelter. • Much biomedical and physiological knowledge can be attributed to laboratory experimentation on these animals. • *R. rattus* (commonly called the black, roof or tree rat) is also found in Southern California. **Where found:** near human habitation; natural habitat preference is in thickly vegetated areas with ample cover, but adapts to every habitat except high mountains; throughout Southern California.

House Mouse

Mus musculus

Length: 5–8 in (tail 2½–4 in)
Weight: ½–¾ oz

This familiar mouse can be
found throughout most of
North America. Like the Norway rat, it arrived
as a stow-away on ships from Europe, quickly spreading across the continent alongside European settlers. The western harvest mouse (*Reithrodontomys megalotis*) looks very similar, though smaller, and is native to North America. • The house mouse is nocturnal in habit and may be responsible for gnawing the labels of the canned soup stored in your cupboards! **Where found:** throughout Southern California, usually associated with human settlements.

Deer Mouse

Peromyscus maniculatus

Length: 5½–8½ in (tail 2–4 in)
Weight: ¾–1¼ oz

Deer mice are seed eaters, but they
will also eat insects, spiders, caterpillars, fungi, flowers and berries.
These mice, in turn, are important prey for many other animal, so must be prolific breeders to maintain their population. A litter of 4–9 young leaves the nest after 3–5 weeks, and the mice are sexually mature 1–2 weeks later. Less than 5% survive a complete year. • The abundant deer mouse is the most widespread *Peromyscus* species in Southern California, but there are several others such as the canyon, cactus, brush and pinyon mice, as well as the California mouse, found mainly on the western fringe of the state. **Where found:** most dry habitats including grasslands, shrublands and forests, as well as urban areas; throughout Southern California.

California Vole

Microtus californicus

Length: 6–8½ in (tail 1½–2½ in)
Weight: 1½–3½ oz

There are many species of vole in California, occupying various habitats and ranges. The best way to encounter a vole is to walk through a grassy field and move aside a large piece of debris, such as an abandoned piece of farm equipment or a fallen log. There will probably be a rapid scattering of little mammals, likely voles. • This vole can occur in significant numbers in California—up to 200 individuals per acre. In areas with a high vole population, the ground is crisscrossed with little pathways like a Los Angeles freeway. **Where found:** various habitats and elevations, including grasslands, grassy slopes, saltwater or freshwater marshes and moist meadows; in the western counties of Southern California.

Long-tailed Pocket Mouse

Chaetodipus formosus

Length: 6¾–8¼ in (tail 3⅜–4⅝ in)
Weight: ½–⅞ oz

Yet another well-adapted nocturnal desert rodent, this species can be distinguished from other pocket mice (which are not really easily distinguishable from other small rodents as they are scurrying quickly out of view) by its long tail. • This desert rodent survives the climatic extremes of its habitat by avoiding them and entering a state of torpor when it gets too hot or too cold. **Where found:** rocky or gravelly sites on slopes and ridges of deserts and canyons; in arid regions of southeastern California.

Botta's Pocket Gopher

Thomomys bottae

Length: 6½–11 in (tail 1½–4 in)
Weight: 2½–9 oz

Although rarely seen in a positive light by most farmers and ranchers, pocket gophers are extremely important in natural areas for their practice of turning up large volumes of soil, thus aerating the ground, cycling soil nutrients and improving water absorption, which improves the growth of plants and reduces the takeover of weedy species. • Pocket gophers' subterranean diet is composed mainly of roots and tubers. • There are 5 species of pocket gophers in California; the most widespread and common is Botta's. **Where found:** a variety of habitats and soil types, from deserts to mountain meadows; throughout Southern California. **Also known as:** valley pocket gopher.

California Ground Squirrel

Spermophilus beecheyi

Length: 14–20 in (tail 5½–8 in)
Weight: 10–26 oz

Although they excavate large burrows that
range from 5–200 ft long, typically under a log,
tree or large boulder, California ground squirrels are also able to climb 20 ft up
a cottonwood tree. • They are non-colonial but will tolerate being part of loose
adult colonies, avoiding the living spaces of their neighbors. At 8 weeks of age, the
young begin to venture away from the nest and dig their own burrows. • This species
is found only in western areas of the state; the round-tailed ground squirrel
(*S. tereticaudus*) is found in the east and the Mohave ground squirrel (*S. mohavensis*)
is endemic to the Mohave Desert. **Where found:** open areas such as pastures, rocky
outcroppings and rolling hills; in western counties of Southern California.

Merriam's Chipmunk

Tamias merriami

Length: 8¼–11 in (tail 3½–5½ in)
Weight: 2½–4 oz

Chipmunks keep busy in the forests of southwestern California, digging burrows that aerate
the soil, feeding on vegetation and insects thus keeping many
weed and pest species in check, and caching seeds that are oftentimes either
forgotten or disregarded, thereby facilitating their dispersal and subsequent
germination. Chipmunks' favorite foods are pinyon pine nuts and acorns, but they
also enjoy nibbling on various flowers and fruits. **Where found:** various habitats,
including rocky areas, brushland and low-elevation coniferous forests; in south-
central California.

Western Gray Squirrel

Sciurus griseus

Length: 18–25 in (tail 9½–12 in)
Weight: 1–2 lb

In true squirrel custom, western gray squirrels are so
nuts about nuts—acorns, hazelnuts and pine nuts—that
they store them in forked tree branches, under fallen logs
or underground, where the nuts often germinate, making this squirrel a fortuitous
gardener. • Western gray squirrels build leafy nests at least 20 ft high in a tree,
often moving into a tree hollow in winter or adverse weather. • Eastern fox squirrels
(*S. niger*) are common in the cities and have a more rusty coloration. **Where found:**
woodlands, especially oak, and frequent inhabitant of backyard trees in urban
environs; along the mountain ranges of Southern California. **Also known as:**
California gray squirrel, Columbian gray squirrel, silver gray squirrel.

White-tailed Antelope Squirrel

Ammospermophilus leucurus

Length: 7⅝–9⅜ in (tail 2⅛–3⅜ in)
Weight: 3–5½ oz

Despite the heat of its arid environment, this little squirrel can be seen actively dashing about the scrub and sand, seemingly playing with other members of its colony. Most of what looks like play, however, is the adults defending their territories; although they live in large aggregations, each adult has its own burrow and, particularly the males, is very aware of social hierarchy. • Food sources include green vegetation, seeds and invertebrates, all of which are also a source of water. **Where found:** deserts, sagebrush scrub and creosote bush scrub of southeastern California.

Northern Flying Squirrel

Glaucomys sabrinus

Length: 9½–15 in (tail 4–7 in)
Weight: 2½–6½ oz

Long flaps of skin stretched between the fore and hind limbs and a broad, flattened tail allow the nocturnal northern flying squirrel to glide swiftly from tree to tree, with extreme glides of up to 110 yards! • This flying squirrel plays an important role in forest ecology because it digs up and eats truffles, the fruiting body of a special ectomycorrhizal fungus that grows underground. Through its stool, the squirrel spreads the beneficial fungus, helping both the fungus and the forest plants. **Where found:** primarily old-growth coniferous and mixed forests; north-central range extends into Kern and San Bernardino counties, with disjunct populations farther south in the state.

Black-tailed Jackrabbit

Lepus californicus

Length: 20–24 in (tail 2½–4 in)
Weight: 5–10 lb

This hare can often be seen at dawn and dusk grazing at roadsides. Although it can run up to 35 mph and leap as far as 20 ft when frightened, the black-tailed jackrabbit still falls prey to eagles, hawks, owls, coyotes and bobcats. • This animal's most prominent features are its large ears, which account for approximately 19% of its total body surface area. This adaptation helps dissipate body heat in the arid climate of Southern California and may also enhance hearing capability, which would aid the animal in avoiding predators. **Where found:** lower-elevation shrublands, sagebrush, fields and grasslands; throughout Southern California.

Brush Rabbit

Sylvilagus bachmani

Length: 11–15 in (tail ½–1½ in)
Weight: 1–2 lb

This tiny rabbit is commonly seen wherever there is some nearby brush for shelter and tender vegetation for food. The brush rabbit feeds on grasses, clover and berries, and incorporates more woody vegetation in its winter diet. This species of rabbit is typically crepuscular, active at dawn and dusk. • Females can have up to 5 litters of 3–4 young per litter in a single year. They raise their young in a fur-lined burrow called a form. **Where found:** low-elevation areas with plenty of brush cover; in the western counties of Southern California.

Desert Cottontail

Sylvilagus audubonii

Length: 15–18 in (tail 1½–2⅜ in)
Weight: 2–2½ lb

These rabbits are most often observed during the hours around sunset and sunrise when they take advantage of the mild temperatures and low-light conditions that their shy nature instinctually prefers, thus avoiding their many predators. Few cottontails live to more than 3 years of age—most fall victim to raptors, coyotes or other large carnivores. To counter high predation rates, cottontails are prolific breeders, as are all rabbits. • Cottontails feed on the succulent tips of grasses, forbs and sagebrush. **Where found:** sagebrush slopes with rocky outcrops and brushy riparian areas; throughout Southern California.

Brazilian Free-tailed Bat

Tadarida brasiliensis

Length: 3½–4½ in (tail 1–2 in)
Wingspan: 11 in (forearm 1½–2 in)
Weight: ¼–½ oz

Brazilian free-tailed bats have impressively large colony sizes, and they vacate their roosts at night in overwhelming numbers. One of the most famous colonies is in the Carlsbad Caverns of New Mexico, which has a population millions strong. Although they do not exist in such great numbers in California, they still are seen exiting caves *en masse*, and large colonies can blanket the ceilings of caves and mines; nursing colonies can have as many as 1500 pups per square foot! **Where found:** crevices, tunnels, mines, caves and vacated buildings; found statewide but migrates south into Mexico in winter. **Also known as:** Mexican free-tailed bat (*T.b. mexicanus*); guano bat.

Western Mastiff Bat

Eumops perotis

Length: 5½–7½ in (tail 1½–3 in)
Wingspan: 20–23 in (forearm 3 in)
Weight: 2¼ oz

This free-tailed bat is the largest in North America. Commonly referred to as the mastiff bat for its pushed-in, pug-like face, which resembles that of a mastiff, this bat actually has quite a delicate face, if you should ever get a close look. • The mastiff bat feeds primarily on moths but also eats crickets and grasshoppers. Its lengthy feeding forays, up to 6–7 hours, might be attributed to its finicky eating habits; this bat plucks the wings, heads and legs off insects before eating them. **Where found:** arid regions with rocky sites or cliffs and canyons for roosting; from mid-coast southward.

Little Brown Bat

Myotis lucifugus

Length: 2½–4 in (tail 1–2 in)
Wingspan: 10 in (forearm 1½ in)
Weight: ¼ oz

These common bats form large maternal roosting colonies each summer to give birth and raise their young, and they are frequently seen flying at night in pursuit of insects or skimming over water sources, such as lakes, ponds and even swimming pools, to get a quick drink. • All the mouse-eared bats (*Myotis* spp.) are generally indistinguishable as they fly in dim light. **Where found:** roosts in buildings, barns, caves, rock crevices, hollow trees and under tree bark; hibernates in buildings, caves and mine adits; throughout Southern California.

Hoary Bat

Lasiurus cinereus

Length: 4–6 in (tail 1½–2½ in)
Wingspan: 16 in (forearm 1¾–2¼ in)
Weight: 1–1¼ oz

This large, beautiful bat roosts in trees, not caves or buildings, and wraps its wings around itself for protection against the elements, its frosty-colored fur blending in amongst the mosses and lichens. The hoary bat also roosts in orchards, but it is an insectivore and does not damage fruit crops. At night, look for its large body and slow wingbeats as it swiftly flies over open terrain. **Where found:** roosts on the branches of coniferous and deciduous trees and occasionally in tree cavities; believed to migrate but destination is unknown; widely distributed, but rarely seen, throughout Southern California.

Western Pipistrelle

Pipistrellus hesperus

Length: 2½–3½ in (tail 1–1¼ in)
Wingspan: 7½–8½ in (forearm 1–1¼ in)
Weight: up to ¼ oz

The western pipistrelle is the smallest bat in the U.S. It is also quite delicate, with a weak, erratic flight style, making it unable to fly in strong wind. Because of its jerky flight, this bat has been given the name "flittermouse" (or *fledermaus* in German) in Europe. • The contrasting black mask, wings and legs against blond fur make this bat distinctively attractive. Whereas most bats produce a single offspring, this species typically produces twins. **Where found:** arid regions with rocky or scrubby areas, sometimes close to cities; roosts in caves or sometimes buildings; throughout Southern California.

Big Brown Bat

Eptesicus fuscus

Length: 3½–5½ in (tail 1–2½ in)
Wingspan: 13 in (forearm 1½–2 in)
Weight: ½–1 oz

Effective for aerial hunting, the big brown bat's ultra-sonic echolocation (80,000–40,000 Hz) can detect flying insects up to 16 ft away. This bat flies above water, around streetlights or over agricultural areas hunting insects at dusk and dawn. • The big brown bat is not abundant but is frequently encountered because of its tendency to roost in human-made structures. It has been known to change hibernation sites in mid-winter, a time when it is extremely rare to spot a bat; it overwinters as far north as Canada. **Where found:** in and around human-made structures; occasionally roosts in hollow trees and rock crevices; throughout Southern California.

Pallid Bat

Antrozous pallidus

Length: 3½–5½ in (tail 1½–2 in)
Wingspan: 15 in (forearm 2–2½ in)
Weight: ½–1¼ oz

The pallid bat is known to grab the occasional insect or other invertebrate (it is known for feeding on scorpions) from the ground, which is unusual and risky behavior. The bat is vulnerable prey itself when on the ground, whereas there are few predators in the night sky. • This bat produces a skunk-like odor from glands on its muzzle when disturbed. **Where found:** rocky outcrops near open, dry areas and, occasionally, evergreen forests; daytime roosts most often in buildings and crevices rather than caves; throughout Southern California.

73

Townsend's Big-eared Bat

Plecotus townsendii

Length: 3½–4½ in (tail 1–2½ in)
Wingspan: 11 in (forearm 1½–2 in)
Weight: ¼–½ oz

Endowed with relatively enormous ears, these rare bats "see" the nighttime world through sound (though all bats have good eyesight, contrary to the blind-as-a-bat myth). Each species of bat is recognizable by the ultrasonic calls it produces, but special equipment is needed to identify bat calls. Bats can hear frequencies as much as 200 times higher than our ears can hear. • This bat feeds almost exclusively on moths. **Where found:** scrub desert, pine and pinyon forests; roosts in caves or buildings; throughout Southern California. **Also known as:** western big-eared bat.

California Leaf-nosed Bat

Macrotus californicus

Length: 3¼–3⅝ in (tail 1¼–1⅝ in)
Wingspan: 13–13½ in (forearm 1⅞–2⅛ in)
Weight: ¼–¾ oz

Steadfastly Californian, this bat does not migrate but remains in the state year-round and endures the cool southeastern winters by roosting in colonies deep in caves. It does not hibernate and even leaves the cave in winter for at least a couple of hours per day to feed on insects. Males form bachelor's roosts outside of the fall breeding season. • This bat is distinctive for being the only one in Southern California that has the ornate leaf-like protuberances on its nose. **Where found:** desert and arid scrub areas of southeastern California.

Broad-footed Mole

Scapanus latimanus

Length: 5–7½ in (tail 1–2 in)
Weight: 2 oz

With little use for eyesight in a life spent underground, the nearly blind broad-footed mole has a sensitive tail and long snout that "see" by feeling as this little mammal burrows through the earth with its strong, paddle-like feet endowed with long, dirt-digging claws. • Another intriguing adaptation to its lifestyle is the mole's velvety fur, which lies flat forward and backward facing, permitting the animal to move in either direction without resistance. **Where found:** soft, moist soils at various elevations; within the western counties of Southern California.

Ornate Shrew

Sorex ornatus

Length: 3⅜–4¼ in (tail 1⅛–1¾ in)
Weight: about ¼ oz

Some species of shrew in
Southern California are
adapted to very specific
and limited habitats, such
as the desert shrew *(Notiosorex crawfordi)* of the southeastern range of the state;
however, the ornate shrew is adaptive enough to inhabit dry upland forests,
marshy inland or coastal salt marsh areas or even open pine forests. • Shrews are
insectivores, and the ornate shrew is no exception; it feeds on various insect species
and their larvae as well as other small invertebrates found under logs, rocks and
leaf litter. • There are several *Sorex* species in California, and they are nearly
impossible to distinguish from each other by mere field observation. They are
nocturnal, they do not hibernate and they nest in wood, shrubs and burrows.
Where found: various habitats including coastal salt marshes, freshwater wetlands, forests and woodlands; southwestern California including a few reports
from Santa Catalina Island.

Virginia Opossum

Didelphis virginiana

Length: 27–33 in (tail 12–14 in)
Weight: 2½–3½ lb

Contrary to most children's stories in
which opossums are portrayed hanging
by their prehensile tails, the Virginia
opossum rarely assumes this posture, though it does climb and den
in trees. It is a marsupial closely
related to kangaroos and koalas.
• The opossum plays dead, a role this
actor is famous for, to convince a potential
attacker to leave it alone. This behavior is
what the expression "playing possum"
derives from. However, playing dead does not
work with cars, which are this slow-moving
nocturnal creature's most common assailant. **Where found:** moist woodlands
or brushy areas near permanent watercourses; the western coast and islands of
Southern California.

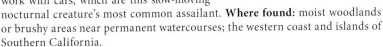

BIRDS

All birds are feathered but not all fly. The most diverse class of vertebrates, birds are bipedal and warm-blooded, and they lay hard-shelled eggs. Some birds migrate south in the colder winter months and return north in spring or migrate north in warm months returning to our area for winter. For this reason, Southern California has a different diversity of birds in summer than in winter. Many migrating birds fly as far south as Central and South America or as far north as the Arctic. Migratory birds are of concern to biologists and conservationists because pesticide use, climate change impacts and decreasing habitat in parts of their range threaten the survival of many species. Education and increasing appreciation for wildlife may encourage solutions to these problems.

Waterfowl
pp. 78–83

Grouse-like Birds
p. 83

Diving Birds
pp. 84–85

Herons & Vultures
pp. 86–87

Birds of Prey
pp. 88–90

Rails & Coots
p. 91

Shorebirds
pp. 92–95

Gulls, Terns
& Skimmers
pp. 96–98

Pigeons & Doves
p. 99

Cuckoos
p. 99

Owls
p. 100

Swifts
p. 100

Hummingbirds & Kingfishers
p. 101

Woodpeckers
p. 102

Flycatchers
p. 103

Vireos
p. 104

Jays & Crows
pp. 104–05

Larks & Swallows
p. 106

Titmice & Nuthatches
pp. 107–08

Wrens, Kinglets & Gnatcatchers
pp. 108–09

Thrushes & Mockingbirds
pp. 109–10

Starlings & Waxwings
p. 111

Wood-warblers & Tanagers
pp. 111–13

Sparrows & Grosbeaks
pp. 114–15

Blackbirds & Allies
pp. 116–17

Finch-like Birds
pp. 117–18

Canada Goose

Branta canadensis

Length: 35–45 in
Wingspan: 4½–6 ft

Canada geese mate for life and are devoted parents to their 2–11 goslings. Wild geese can be aggressive when defending young or competing for food. Hissing sounds and low, outstretched necks are signs to give these birds some space. • Geese graze on aquatic grasses and sprouts, and you can spot them tipping up to grab for aquatic roots and tubers. • The Canada goose was split into 2 species in 2004; the smaller subspecies have been renamed the "cackling goose." **Where found:** lakeshores, ponds, parks, marshes and croplands; widespread winter resident.

Mallard

Anas platyrhynchos

Length: 20–28 in
Wingspan: 3 ft

The male mallard, with his shiny, green head and chestnut brown breast, is the classic wild duck, and this duck species is one of the only ones that really "quacks." • The female incubates 7–10 creamy, grayish or greenish white eggs in a grass nest built on the ground, sometimes under a bush. Mallards readily hybridize with a variety of other duck species, including barnyard ducks, often producing offspring with very peculiar plumages. **Where found:** lakes, wetlands, rivers, city parks, agricultural areas, sewage lagoons and even outdoor swimming pools; widespread year-round.

Northern Pintail

Anas acuta

Length: *Male:* 25–30 in; *Female:* 20–22 in
Wingspan: *Male:* 34 in; *Female:* 34 in

Its long neck and long, tapered tail put this dabbling duck in a class of its own. The elegant and graceful northern pintail occurs in Asia and northern Europe, as well as in North America. • These migrants move through the state early to scout out flooded agricultural fields farther north for choice nesting locations. Unfortunately, northern pintails usually build their nests in vulnerable areas, on exposed ground near water, which has resulted in a slow decline in their population. **Where found:** shallow wetlands, flooded fields and lake edges; widespread, but found only in the extreme southeast in winter.

Cinnamon Teal

Anas cyanoptera

Length: 15–16 in
Wingspan: 20–22 in

Cinnamon teals are one of the few species of duck that commonly nest in Southern California. • The males sport the attractive auburn plumage that draws attention to this species; the duck, however, is not seeking attention and often paddles along with its head partially submerged as it searches for a meal of invertebrates. • Cinnamon teals are often seen swimming in a row as those in file feed on the invertebrates churned up by the paddling feet of the leader. **Where found:** freshwater ponds, marshes, sloughs and flooded swales; year-round resident of the western cismontane, but typically found only in the Inland Empire in summer.

Northern Shoveler

Anas clypeata

Length: 18–20 in
Wingspan: 30 in

An extra large, spoon-like bill allows the northern shoveler to strain small invertebrates from the water and from the bottoms of ponds. This specialized feeding
strategy means that the duck is rarely seen tipping up but is more likely found in
the shallows of ponds and marshes where the mucky bottom is easiest to access.
Where found: shallow marshes, bogs and lakes with muddy bottoms and emergent
vegetation, usually in open and semi-open areas, and along the coast in sheltered
areas; widespread winter resident.

American Wigeon

Anas americana

Length: 18–23 in
Wingspan: 34 in

From October to May, this dabbler is a familiar visitor to backyards, parks and
golf courses as well as its natural habitat in grassy wetlands. The male is easily
identifiable by his head markings, which look like a common male balding pattern
with a ring of green on an otherwise bald head. The pale blue-gray bill is also
distinguishable. The female duck, like most other species, is drab in color. **Where
found:** marshes and shallow lakes with emergent or lush bordering vegetation,
intertidal eelgrass beds, fresh or upper-estuarine waters and protected coastal
waters; widespread winter resident.

Lesser Scaup

Aythya affinis

Length: 15–18 in
Wingspan: 25 in

A tri-color appearance makes this widespread diving duck easy to recognize and remember; it is often described with the analogy of an Oreo cookie—a white center between 2 dark ends. The lesser scaup has a small white inner wing stripe visible in flight that becomes dull gray on the primaries, and the male has a purple, peaked head. • This diving duck is graceful in the water, but on land and when taking flight it is awkward and clumsy owing to its short wings and the placement of its legs well back on its body; these adaptations make diving more efficient, but even a novice birder will identify a diving duck as it runs, flapping its wings, along the water's surface in its efforts to fly. **Where found:** deep, open fresh and estuarine waters, lakes, harbors, estuaries and lagoons in winter and migration; widespread.

Surf Scoter

Melanitta perspicillata

Length: 17–21 in
Wingspan: 28–31 in

The surf scoter sits like a sturdy buoy on the waves of bays, inlets and large lakes. This bird breeds in Alaska and northern Canada and is well adapted for life on rough waters, spending winters just beyond the breaking surf on the Atlantic and Pacific coasts. Although the surf scoter is the only scoter that breeds and over-winters exclusively on this continent, it is largely unstudied. • The surf scoter dives underwater to feed on mussels and crustaceans, and it can be observed diving, as if playing, through the breaking surf. **Where found:** bays and inlets along the coast.

Bufflehead

Bucephala albeola

Length: 13–15 in
Wingspan: 21 in

The typical bufflehead spends its entire life in North America; its breeding grounds are in the boreal forests of Canada and Alaska, and it winters primarily in marine bays and estuaries along the Atlantic and Pacific coasts. Many of these ducks migrate through our region, and a few stay on to overwinter on our larger lakes and rivers. • Fish, crustaceans and mollusks make up a major portion of the bufflehead's winter diet, but in summer, this duck eats large amounts of aquatic invertebrates and tubers. **Where found:** open water on lakes, large ponds and rivers; widespread winter resident.

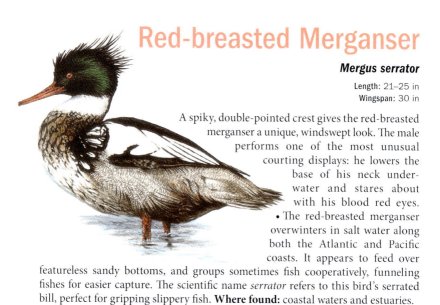

Red-breasted Merganser

Mergus serrator

Length: 21–25 in
Wingspan: 30 in

A spiky, double-pointed crest gives the red-breasted merganser a unique, windswept look. The male performs one of the most unusual courting displays: he lowers the base of his neck under-water and stares about with his blood red eyes. • The red-breasted merganser overwinters in salt water along both the Atlantic and Pacific coasts. It appears to feed over featureless sandy bottoms, and groups sometimes fish cooperatively, funneling fishes for easier capture. The scientific name *serrator* refers to this bird's serrated bill, perfect for gripping slippery fish. **Where found:** coastal waters and estuaries.

Ruddy Duck

Owyura jamaicensis

Length: 15–16 in
Wingspan: 18–19 in

The male ruddy duck's red feathers and large, blue bill make this duck eye-catching and unforgettably endearing. With a bill-pumping display followed by staccato grunting as he courts a mate, he further draws our attention. • The ruddy duck dives underwater to feed, propelled by large feet set far back on its body. **Where found:** widespread year-round. *Breeding:* large, deepwater marshes and the margins of reed-skirted ponds. *Nonbreeding:* birds assemble in large flocks on still or protected tidal waters.

California Quail

Callipepla californica

Length: 10–11 in
Wingspan: 14 in

First introduced to our area in the 1800s, though largely absent from the coast, the California quail is a year-round resident in low-elevation brushy habitats and parks. It is seen scuttling about in tight, cohesive flocks that can sometimes have up to 200 birds. This bird's unmistakable feature is the truly cute head plumage. • It typically falls prey to feral cats, but most predatory birds and mammals would make an effort to catch this plump meal. **Where found:** chaparral, brush, suburban parks and oak and riparian woodland regions; widespread year-round.

BIRDS

Pacific Loon

Gavia pacifica

Length: 23–29 in
Wingspan: 41–49 in

From mid-April through May, hundreds of thousands of these arctic breeders can be observed in great flocks as they head north, leaving behind California's warm summer shore for cooler climes and returning in fall to spend the winter here or on the Sea of Cortez. They can be observed from select shore points, but they prefer the open ocean to the upper-estuarine waters, avoiding the rough surfline. **Where found:** winter resident in coastal ocean waters, including harbors and bays, or often in the immediate lee of a headland or jetty.

Pied-billed Grebe

Podilymbus podiceps

Length: 12–15 in
Wingspan: 16 in

Relatively solid bones and the ability to partially deflate its air sac allow the pied-billed grebe to sink below the surface of the water like a tiny submarine. • Although local populations stay here year-round, on fall evenings, an influx of the migrant populations of these grebes can be seen returning to the ponds, lakes and estuaries where they spend winter. **Where found:** widespread year-round. *Breeding*: deep, freshwater lakes, ponds and other water sources. *Nonbreeding*: varied open and semi-open fresh and estuarine waters and kelp beds.

Eared Grebe

Podiceps nigricollis

Length: 11½–14 in
Wingspan: 16 in

Eared grebes undergo cyclical periods of atrophy and hypertrophy of their internal organs and pectoral muscles, depending on whether or not the birds need to migrate. This strategy leaves eared grebes flightless for up to 10 months annually—longer than any other flying bird in the world. • In Southern California we do not see the golden "ears" of this bird's breeding plumage; the northeastern border of the state marks the edge of the interior summer ranges of this grebe. The birds stage in large numbers on alkaline lakes in California. **Where found:** coastal waters, lagoons, open estuaries, interior lakes, reservoirs, ponds and slow rivers; winter resident along the western coastal fringe of the state.

84

Western Grebe

Aechmophorus occidentalis

Length: 25 in
Wingspan: 24 in

Elegant western grebes are famous for their elaborate courtship rituals, in which pairs caress each other with aquatic vegetation and sprint side by side, literally walking on water. The breeding pair builds a floating nest of wet vegetation anchored to submerged plants and incubates 2–4 eggs. The hatchlings climb directly from the egg onto the parents' backs. **Where found:** prefers large waterbodies, both freshwater and marine; coastal and lakes or other large water bodies near the coast in winter.

Brown Pelican

Pelecanus occidentalis

Length: 4 ft
Wingspan: 7 ft

With even wing beats, brown pelicans fly gracefully above sunbathers and boaters, but then dive bomb head first with folded wings into the water, to depths of up to 60 ft, to catch fish. • In the 1950s and 1960s, DDT-related reproductive failures caused brown pelicans to nearly disappear in many areas of the southeastern U.S. Since these highly persistent pesticides were banned in the 1970s, pelican populations have recovered. **Where found:** visits offshore islands; roosts on protected islets, sea stacks, sandbars and piers; year-round in coastal and estuarine waters.

Double-crested Cormorant

Phalacrocorax auritus

Length: 26–32 in
Wingspan: 4¼ ft

The double-crested cormorant looks like a bird but swims, and smells, like a fish. With a long, rudder-like tail, excellent underwater vision, sealed nostrils for diving and "wettable" feathers (lacking oil glands), this bird has mastered the underwater world. • The cormorant often perches with its wings partially spread. It is a colonial nester and builds its nest on a platform of sticks and guano. • A traditional Japanese fishing method called *ukai* employs cormorants on leashes to catch fish. **Where found:** large lakes and large, meandering rivers; nests on islands or in trees; along the coast year-round.

Great Blue Heron

Ardea herodias

Length: 4¼–4½ ft
Wingspan: 6 ft

The long-legged great blue heron employs a stealthy, often motionless hunting strategy. It waits for a fish or frog to approach, spears the prey with its bill, then flips its catch into the air and swallows it whole. This heron usually hunts near water, but it also stalks fields and meadows in search of rodents. • The great blue heron settles in communal treetop nests called rookeries, and nest width can reach 4 ft. **Where found:** forages along edges of rivers, lakes and marshes; also in fields and meadows; widespread year-round.

Great Egret

Ardea alba

Length: 3–3½ ft
Wingspan: 4 ft

The plumes of great egrets and snowy egrets were widely used to decorate hats in the early 20th century. Some of the first conservation legislation in North America was enacted to outlaw the hunting of great egrets; the great egret is the symbol for the National Audubon Society, one of the oldest conservation organizations in the United States. **Where found:** marshes, open riverbanks, irrigation canals and lakeshores; nests in dense tree stands; widespread year-round.

Snowy Egret

Egretta thula

Length: 22–26 in
Wingspan: 3½ ft

Looking as if it stepped in a can of yellow paint, the dainty snowy egret flaunts famously yellow feet on black legs. Come breeding season, the egret's lores and feet turn a deeper orange, and long plumes—perhaps the most sought-after for the plume trade—extend from its neck and back. • Snowy egrets teetered on the brink of extirpation from our region by the early 1900s but have recovered dramatically and now occur beyond their historical range limits. **Where found:** edges of marshes, rivers, lakes and ponds; flooded agricultural fields; widespread on or near the coast year-round, but observed in the Inland Empire typically only in summer.

Black-crowned Night-heron

Nycticorax nycticorax

Length: 23–26 in
Wingspan: 3½ ft

When dusk's long shadows shroud the marshes,
the black-crowned night-herons arrive to hunt
in the marshy waters. These herons crouch motionless,
using their large, light-sensitive eyes to spot prey lurking in   the shallows.
• Black-crowned night-herons breed throughout much of the United States and
are the most abundant herons in the world, occurring virtually worldwide. Watch
for them in summer, between dawn and dusk, as they fly from nesting colonies to
feeding areas and back. **Where found:** shallow cattail and bulrush marshes, lakeshores and along slow rivers and along the coast; widespread year-round.

Turkey Vulture

Cathartes aura

Length: 25–31 in
Wingspan: 5½–6 ft

The turkey vulture is a playful, social bird, and
groups live and sleep together in large trees,
or roosts. Some roost sites are over a century old and have been used by the same family of
vultures for several generations. • No other bird uses
updrafts and thermals in flight as well as the turkey vulture. Pilots have reported
seeing this vulture soaring at 20,000 ft. **Where found:** usually flies over open country, shorelines or roads but rarely over forests; widespread year-round in coastal
regions, but found inland only in summer.

California Condor

Gymnogyps californianus

Length: 3½–4½ ft
Wingspan: 8½–9½ ft

The massive California condor has become an emblem of
the complexities of wildlife conservation. Once ranging
across the country, its decline since the beginning of
European settlement is the result of shooting, poisoning,
egg collection, nest harassment and food scarcity. The
last wild condor went into captivity in 1987, and today,
all condors are captive bred and released into uncertain futures. They have been
reintroduced to the coastal mountains of south-central California and the Grand
Canyon area of northern Arizona. Condors are a marked, radio-tagged and
intensely managed remnant species, unable to fulfill any meaningful ecological
role today. **Where found:** arid foothills, mountains and canyons with updrafts for
soaring; in the coastal mountains.

White-tailed Kite

Elanus leucurus

Length: 15–17 in
Wingspan: 3¼ ft

This dedicated hunter seeks prey from early morning until twilight. When it spots a target, such as a vole scurrying in the grass, it drops to the earth with its wings held high like a parachute. The white-tailed kite flies with a grace and buoyancy uncommon among raptors. • Evening roosts in winter sometimes number over 100 birds. • Formerly known as the "black-shouldered kite," this bird's numbers are now strong in western California after near extirpation from the state in the early 20th century. **Where found:** year-round in tree-dotted lowlands, hillside fields, non-grazed grasslands and marshes of the western cismontane.

Northern Harrier

Circus cyaneus

Length: 16–24 in
Wingspan: 3½–4 ft

The courtship flight of the northern harrier is a spring spectacle worth watching. The male climbs almost vertically in the air, then stalls and plummets in a reckless dive toward the ground. At the last second, he saves himself with a hairpin turn that sends him skyward again. • Britain's Royal Air Force named the Harrier aircraft after this bird for its impressive maneuverability. **Where found:** open country; fields, wet meadows, cattail marshes, bogs and croplands; nests on the ground, usually in tall vegetation; widespread in winter.

Cooper's Hawk

Accipiter cooperii

Length: *Male:* 15–17 in; *Female:* 17–19 in
Wingspan: *Male:* 27–32 in; *Female:* 32–37 in

Cooper's hawk will quickly change the scene at a backyard bird feeder when it comes looking for a meal.
European starlings, American robins and house sparrows are among its favorite choices of prey. When
there are no feeders in the area, it hunts along forest
edges. With the help of its short, square tail and flap-
and-glide flight, it is capable of maneuvering
quickly at high speeds to snatch its prey in mid-air.
The sharp-shinned hawk (*A. striatus*) is a similar
species in form and habit but is only present in winter in
most of Southern California, whereas Cooper's hawk is
found year-round in most of its Southern Californian
range and habitat. **Where found:** mixed and riparian
woodlands and urban gardens with feeders; nests in trees,
often near a stream or pond; widespread year-round.

Red-shouldered Hawk

Buteo lineatus

Length: 19 in
Wingspan: 3½ ft

The red-shouldered hawk nests in mature trees, usually
in river bottoms and lowland tracts of woods alongside creeks. As spring approaches and pair bonds are
formed, this normally quiet hawk utters loud, shrieking
key-ah calls. If left undisturbed, the red-shouldered
hawk will remain faithful to productive nesting
sites, returning yearly for generations. **Where
found:** mature deciduous and mixed forests, swampy
woodlands, coastal bottomlands, agricultural lands,
suburbs and city parks, lightly wooded foothills
and unmanaged riversides; does not range far
from the coast; observed year-round.

Red-tailed Hawk

Buteo jamaicensis

Length: *Male:* 18–23 in; *Female:* 20–25 in
Wingspan: 4–5 ft

Spend a summer afternoon in the country, and you will likely see a red-tailed hawk perched on a fence post or soaring on thermals. • Courting red-tails will sometimes dive at one another, lock talons and tumble toward the earth, breaking away at the last second to avoid crashing into the ground. • The red-tailed hawk's piercing call is often paired with the image of an eagle in TV commercials and movies. **Where found:** roadsides, woodlots and open country with some trees; can often be seen flying above cities; widespread year-round.

American Kestrel

Falco sparverius

Length: 7½–8 in
Wingspan: 20–24 in

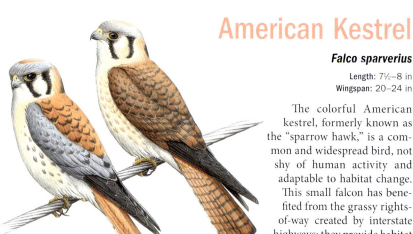

The colorful American kestrel, formerly known as the "sparrow hawk," is a common and widespread bird, not shy of human activity and adaptable to habitat change. This small falcon has benefited from the grassy rights-of-way created by interstate highways; they provide habitat for grasshoppers, which make up most of its diet, as well as other small prey such as mice. **Where found:** along rural roads, perched on poles and telephone wires; agricultural and open fields, grasslands, riparian woodlands, woodlots, forest edges, bogs, roadside ditches and grassy highway medians; widespread year-round.

Sora

Porzana carolina

Length: 8–10 in
Wingspan: 14 in

The sora has a small body and large, chicken-like feet. Even without webbed feet, this unique creature swims quite well over short distances. • Two rising *or-Ah or-Ah* whistles followed by a strange, descending whinny indicate that a sora is nearby. Although the sora is the most common and widespread rail species in North America, it is seldom seen. This secretive bird prefers to remain hidden in dense marshland, but it will occasionally venture into the shallows to search for aquatic insects and mollusks. • A well-built basket nest made of grass and aquatic vegetation is where a pair of soras incubate 10–12 eggs for 18–20 days. **Where found:** wetlands with abundant emergent cattails, bulrushes, sedges and grasses; throughout Southern California year-round.

American Coot

Fulica americana

Length: 13–16 in
Wingspan: 24 in

This bird's behavior during the breeding season confirms the expression, "crazy as a coot." It is aggressively territorial and constantly squabbles with other water birds in its space. • With feet that have individually webbed toes, the coot is adapted to diving, but it also isn't afraid to steal a meal from another skilled diver when a succulent piece of water celery is brought to the surface. **Where found:** shallow marshes, ponds and wetlands with open water and emergent vegetation, sewage lagoons and inshore kelp beds; throughout Southern California year-round.

Black-bellied Plover

Pluvialis squatarola

Length: 10½–13 in
Wingspan: 29 in

Black-bellied plovers may be seen along the coast in winter, roosting in tight flocks or running along the mudflats when the tide goes out. These large plovers forage for small invertebrates with a robin-like run-and-stop technique, frequently pausing to lift their heads for a reassuring scan of their surroundings. • Watch for small flocks flashing their bold white wing stripes as they fly low over the water's surface. **Where found:** coastal mudflats and beaches, plowed fields, sod farms, meadows and the edges of lakeshores and reservoirs of coastal Southern California; winter coastal resident.

Killdeer

Charadrius vociferus

Length: 9–11 in
Wingspan: 24 in

The killdeer is a gifted actor, well known for its "broken wing" distraction display. When an intruder wanders too close to its nest (on open ground in a shallow, usually unlined depression), the killdeer greets the interloper with piteous cries while dragging a wing and stumbling about as if injured. Most predators take the bait and follow, and once the killdeer has lured the predator far away from its nest, it miraculously recovers from the injury and flies off with a loud call. **Where found:** open, wet meadows, lakeshores, sandy beaches, mudflats, gravel streambeds and golf courses; widespread year-round resident.

Black-necked Stilt

Himantopus mexicanus

Length: 14–15 in
Wingspan: 29 in

Extraordinarily long, stilt-like legs make this bird an exceptional wader. Proportionally, it has the longest legs of any North American bird. • The black-necked stilt uses its long, needle-like bill to pick insects, crustaceans and other aquatic invertebrates from the water's surface or to probe the substrate for prey. **Where found:** along the margins of freshwater, brackish or saltwater marshes and marshy shorelines of lakes, ponds and tidal mudflats; may be a year-round resident in small, localized populations in the very southwest corner of the state and patchily up the coast; otherwise uncommon in winter when most migrate down into Baja California.

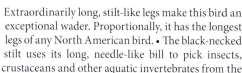

American Avocet

Recurvirostra americana

Length: 17–18 in
Wingspan: 31 in

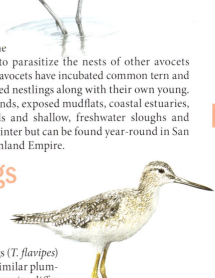

An American avocet in full breeding plumage, with a peachy red head and neck, needle-like bill and black and white body, paints an elegant picture against the mudflats. • Females have been known to parasitize the nests of other avocets and perhaps of other species. Conversely, avocets have incubated common tern and black-necked stilt eggs, raising the adopted nestlings along with their own young. **Where found:** lakeshores, alkaline wetlands, exposed mudflats, coastal estuaries, shallow lagoons, salt evaporation ponds and shallow, freshwater sloughs and ponds; typically near or on the coast in winter but can be found year-round in San Diego County; summer resident of the Inland Empire.

Greater Yellowlegs

Tringa melanoleuca

Length: 13–15 in
Wingspan: 28 in

The greater yellowlegs and lesser yellowlegs (*T. flavipes*) are medium-sized sandpipers with very similar plumages and very yellow legs and feet. The species differ only subtly, and a solitary greater yellowlegs is difficult to identify until it flushes and utters its distinctive 3 peeps (the lesser yellowlegs peeps twice). As its name suggests, the greater yellowlegs is the larger species, and it has a longer, slightly upturned bill. **Where found:** any type of shallow wetland, whether freshwater, brackish or salt, and flooded agricultural fields; widespread winter resident.

Willet

Catoptrophorus semipalmatus

Length: 14–16 in
Wingspan: 26 in

Though plain and inconspicuous at rest, willets are striking in flight, revealing a bold black and white wing pattern when they open their wings. • They are commonly found in flocks of dozens of individuals, often towering over the other shorebirds and uttering loud *pill-will-willet* calls. When feeding, willets often spread out, but when one bird takes flight, the entire flock calls to each other and follows suit. **Where found:** brackish and saline marshes, beaches and flooded agricultural fields; widespread winter resident of the western cismontane.

Black Turnstone

Arenaria melanocephala

Length: 9 in
Wingspan: 21 in

Turnstones got their names from their foraging technique of turning over stones and other loose objects in search of small crustaceans and mollusks such as barnacles and limpets. • Black turnstones retain a dark plumage year-round and are common all along our coastline in winter, but they do not nest here. They are seen in small flocks, displaying aggressive behavior toward each other and other species. **Where found:** rocky shorelines, breakwaters, jetties and reefs; may visit beaches with seaweed wracks as well as mudflats, gravel bars and temporary ponds; coastal winter resident.

Sanderling

Calidris alba

Length: 7–8½ in
Wingspan: 17 in

This charismatic shorebird graces sandy shorelines around the world. The sanderling chases the waves in and out, snatching up aquatic invertebrates before they are swept back into the water. On shores where wave action is limited, it resorts to probing mudflats for a meal of mollusks and insects. • To keep warm, the sanderling seeks the company of roosting sandpipers or plovers and turnstones. It will also take a rest from its zigzag dance along a beach to stand with one leg tucked up, a posture that conserves body heat. **Where found:** sandy and muddy shorelines, cobble and pebble beaches, spits, lakeshores, marshes and reservoirs; coastal winter resident.

Western Sandpiper

Calidris mauri

Length: 6–7 in
Wingspan: 14 in

The western sandpiper is a member of a group of sandpipers known as "peeps" in North America and "stints" elsewhere in the English-speaking world. All peeps are similar in plumage but they are recognized as a group by their exuberant aerial maneuvers as flocks wheel over estuarine tidal flats. • Western sandpipers breed only in Alaska and extreme northeastern Siberia but pass through our area in large numbers in migration and are seen on most of our coast in winter. **Where found:** tidal estuaries, saltwater marshes, sandy beaches, freshwater shorelines, flooded fields and pool; widespread.

Dunlin

Calidris alpina

Length: 7–9 in
Wingspan: 17 in

The Dunlin is a common winter shorebird and can often be seen in very large flocks at tide-line roosts. • Its winter plumage, when we observe it, is unfortunately rather drab, but by spring, just before it gets ready to migrate, you may start to see some of its more attractive summer wear of lovely russet plumage on its back and a bold black belly. • The Dunlin is a swift mover, speed being essential to escape predators. **Where found:** tidal and saltwater marshes, estuaries and lagoon shorelines, open sandy ocean beaches, flooded fields and muddy wetlands; coastal winter resident and migrant through the interior.

Wilson's Snipe

Gallinago delicata

Length: 10½–11½ in
Wingspan: 18 in

When flushed from cover, snipes perform a series of aerial zigzags to confuse predators. Because of this habit, hunters who were skilled enough to shoot snipes became known as "snipers," a term later adopted by the military. • Courting snipes make an eerie, winnowing sound, like a rapidly hooting owl. The male's specialized outer tail feathers vibrate rapidly in the air as he performs daring, headfirst dives high above a wetland. • The female incubates 4 eggs for 18–20 days, but both parents raise the snipe nestlings, often splitting the brood between them. **Where found:** cattail and bulrush marshes, willow and red-osier dogwood tangles, sedge meadows, poorly drained floodplains, bogs and fens; widespread winter resident.

Heerman's Gull

Larus heermanni

Length: 16–18 in
Wingspan: 4 ft

While most gulls are difficult to distinguish from each other, Heerman's gull stands out with a unique style even as a juvenile. It also differs from other gulls in its migration patterns and can be seen in California year-round. Whereas most gulls migrate north to breed and only return south for winter, Heerman's gull heads south in early spring to breed and nest, often on the islands in the Sea of Cortez, and returns by mid-June, sticking around at least until December. • Heerman's gull is commonly observed stealing food from the bills of other birds, such as brown pelicans. **Where found:** all along the coastline in bays, harbors, beaches and offshore islands.

Ring-billed Gull

Larus delawarensis

Length: 18–20 in
Wingspan: 4 ft

Few people can claim that they have never seen these common, widespread gulls. Highly tolerant of humans, ring-billed gulls will eat almost anything as they swarm parks, beaches, golf courses and fast-food parking lots looking for food handouts and often making pests of themselves. However, few species have adjusted to human development as well as this gull, which is something to appreciate. • To differentiate between gulls, pay attention to the markings on their bills and the color of their legs and eyes. **Where found:** a wide spectrum of open country foraging environments relatively close to water; common at garbage dumps; widespread winter resident.

California Gull

Larus californicus

Length: 18–20 in
Wingspan: 4–4½ ft

Despite its name, the California gull was a celebrated hero in Utah when it ate hordes of crop-threatening grasshoppers in 1848 and 1855. There is a monument in Salt Lake City honoring this gull, which is now the Utah state bird. • The world's largest colony of California gulls is at Mono Lake. **Where found:** lakes, marshes, croplands, estuaries and open ocean to miles offshore; cities and garbage dumps; winter resident on the coast and into the western slopes of the coastal mountains.

Western Gull

Larus occidentalis

Length: 24–26 in
Wingspan: 5 ft

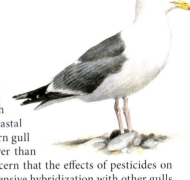

This bird is "the" Pacific Coast seagull—one cannot overlook its conspicuous size and presence. It is a year-round resident on much of our coastline and is a colonial nester on coastal rocks with some vegetative cover. The western gull is not large in numbers, however, with fewer than 200 breeding colonies in total. There is concern that the effects of pesticides on reproduction, threats from oil spills and extensive hybridization with other gulls is compromising its population status. **Where found:** year-round coastal resident on offshore rocks, in intertidal and shallow inshore zones, open ocean upwellings, coastal fields and coastal towns.

Caspian Tern

Sterna caspia

Length: 19–23 in
Wingspan: 4–4½ ft

The North American Caspian tern population has dramatically increased in the last half-century, mainly because of nesting habitat provided by human-made dredge-spoil islands and dikes. • Adults ferociously defend breeding colonies, aggressively attacking and dive-bombing potential predators, and are extremely sensitive to disturbance—birdwatchers are advised to keep their distance. • This tern is believed to live an average of 12 years, but the oldest wild Caspian tern lived more than 26 years! • The Caspian tern is the largest tern in the world. **Where found:** beaches, mudflats, sandbars, lakes and flooded agricultural fields; year-round coastal resident.

Forster's Tern

Sterna forsteri

Length: 14–16 in
Wingspan: 31 in

Forster's tern so closely resembles the common tern (S. hirundo) that the two often seem indistinguishable to the eyes of many observers. • Forster's tern has an exclusively North American breeding distribution, but it bears the name of a man who never visited this continent: German naturalist Johann Reinhold Forster (1729–98). Forster, who lived and worked in England, examined tern specimens sent from Hudson Bay, Canada, and recognized this bird as a distinct species. **Where found:** coastal areas, brackish wetlands and freshwater lakes, rivers and marshes; coastal winter resident.

Least Tern

Sterna antillarum

Length: 9 in
Wingspan: 20 in

With a hearty appetite for fish, the least tern sticks close to water, breeding locally along our coast then migrating to Central and South America for the winter. Unfortunately, much of this endangered bird's breeding habitat has been lost to development and disturbance. Like many colonial water birds, breeding success varies annually in response to food supply, weather, predation and disturbance. • Terns are known for their elaborate courtship displays, which include distinctive calls, flights and parading. While displaying a fish in its beak, a breeding male will lead several other terns in a dramatic aerial performance. The ritual reaches a climax when the female tern accepts the male's offering of fish. **Where found:** builds colonial scrape nests on flat ground, sand islands, sandbars or a flat rooftop near large lakes and rivers; on or near the coast in summer.

Black Skimmer

Rynchops niger

Length: 18 in
Wingspan: 44 in

The black skimmer is the only bird in North America with a lower mandible that is longer than its upper mandible. The skimmer plows its scoop-like lower mandible just below the water's surface feeling for fish, then slams its upper mandible down, clamping the slippery prey securely within its bill. • The unmistakable black skimmer propels itself through the air on long, swept-back wings, flying low over shallow water. **Where found:** coastal marine habitats including estuaries, lagoons, sheltered bays and inlets; in the far south of the state year-round.

Rock Pigeon

Columba livia

Length: 12–13 in
Wingspan: 28 in; male is usually larger

This pigeon is likely a descendant of a Eurasian bird that was first domesticated about 4500 BC. Both Caesar and Napoleon used rock pigeons as message couriers. European settlers introduced the rock pigeon to North America in the 17th century, and today, it is familiar to most anyone who has lived in a city. • No other "wild" bird varies as much in coloration, a result of semi-domestication and extensive inbreeding over time. **Where found:** urban areas, railway yards and agricultural areas; high cliffs often provide more natural habitat; widespread year-round. **Also known as:** rock dove.

Mourning Dove

Zenaida macroura

Length: 11–13 in
Wingspan: 18 in

The mourning dove's soft cooing, which filters through broken woodlands and suburban parks, is often confused with the sound of a hooting owl. • This dove is one of the most abundant native birds in North America, with increased numbers and range since human development created more open habitats and food sources, such as waste grain and bird feeders. • Mourning doves lay only 2 eggs at a time but can have up to 6 broods each year—more than any other native bird. **Where found:** open and riparian woodlands, forest edges, agricultural and suburban areas and parks; widespread year-round.

Greater Roadrunner

Geococcyx californianus

Length: 23 in
Wingspan: 22 in

Celebrated for its appearance, speed and ability to catch rattlesnakes, the greater roadrunner is one of our region's most fascinating birds. This terrestrial member of the cuckoo family runs on spindly legs at speeds of up to 17 mph, chasing after small rodents, lizards, scorpions and insects. Lightning swiftness allows the roadrunner to snatch hummingbirds, bats and rattlesnakes, which are slammed repeatedly against the ground and then consumed. Because their carnivorous diet has a high water content, roadrunners are able survive if water is not readily available. **Where found:** agricultural lands, thorn forests, desert and arid woodlands of pinyon-pine and juniper; widespread throughout arid habitats.

Barn Owl

Tyto alba

Length: 12½–18 in
Wingspan: 3¾ ft

People and barn owls have a mutually beneficial relationship: we provide roosting and nesting structures, such as barns, and open hunting habitat, such as croplands, and in return, these dedicated hunters keep rodent populations down. Their tolerance of and affiliation with human activity make them the most likely owls you will encounter. **Where found:** roosts and nests in cliffs, hollow trees, barns, mine shafts, caves, bridges and similar locations; requires open areas such as agricultural fields, pastures, lawns, marshy meadows, open beaches or open streamside areas for hunting; widespread year-round.

Great Horned Owl

Bubo virginianus

Length: 18–25 in
Wingspan: 3–5 ft

This highly adaptable and superbly camouflaged hunter has sharp hearing and powerful vision that allow it to hunt by night and day. It will swoop down from a perch onto almost any small creature that moves. • The leading edge of the flight feathers is fringed rather than smooth, which interrupts airflow over the wing and allows the owl to fly noiselessly. • The great horned owl has a poor sense of smell, which might explain why it is the only consistent predator of skunks. **Where found:** fragmented forests, fields, riparian woodlands, suburban parks and wooded edges of landfills; widespread year-round.

White-throated Swift

Aeronautes saxatalis

Length: 6–7 in
Wingspan: 15 in

The white-throated swift is a true aeronaut (*Aeronautes* means "sky sailor")—only brief, cliff-clinging rest periods and annual nesting duties bring it to earth. This bird feeds, drinks, bathes and even mates while flying. As its name suggests, the swift is fast; it has been clocked at up to 200 mph—fast enough to avoid the talons of hungry falcons. **Where found:** *Breeding:* high cliffs, crags and dry escarpments in open country surrounded by coniferous forest; high desert fault blocks and river canyons; ranges widely in search of food. *In migration:* also at lower elevations; widespread year-round.

Anna's Hummingbird

Calypte anna

Length: 3–4 in
Wingspan: 5–5½ in

The eye-catching rose-red head of the male Anna's hummingbird makes it the most distinctive "hummer" in Southern California. Though there are other species in our area, no other hummingbird on the continent can compete with this little gem as far as plumage is concerned. • Hummingbirds seek nectar from flowers but will occasionally eat insects; Anna's hummingbird eats more arthropods than most other species of hummer. **Where found:** warm, semi-open, lightly wooded country outside of the high mountains; retreats to lowlands and towns in winter; fairly common year-round resident of the western cismontane (west of the mountain ranges) and extending east along the counties of San Diego and Imperial.

Allen's Hummingbird

Selasphorus sasin

Length: 3½ in
Wingspan: 4½ in

The male Allen's hummingbird could be perceived as over-compensating for his small stature when he is observed staking out his breeding territory: he is quick to establish his territory and perches on high branches of bushes and trees to get a clear vantage point from which to guard his domain. • Hummingbirds are able to fly vertically and in reverse. In forward flight, they beat their wings up to 80 times per second, and their hearts can beat up to 1200 times per minute! **Where found:** nearly any habitat with abundant flowers including gardens, woodland edges, coastal sage scrub, burned sites, brushy slopes and alpine meadows; widespread throughout the western cismontane; becoming a nearly year-round resident in Southern California.

Belted Kingfisher

Ceryle alcyon

Length: 11–14 in
Wingspan: 20–21 in

Perched on a bare branch over a productive pool, the kingfisher plunges headfirst into the water, snatches up a fish or a frog, flips it into the air then swallows it headfirst. Nestlings are able to swallow small fish whole at only 5 days old. • In Greek mythology, Alcyon, the daughter of the wind god, grieved so deeply for her drowned husband that the gods transformed them both into kingfishers. **Where found:** rivers, large streams, lakes, marshes and beaver ponds, especially near exposed soil banks, gravel pits or bluffs; widespread winter resident but may be observed year-round in the north of its range.

Acorn Woodpecker

Melanerpes formicivorus

Length: 9 in
Wingspan: 15–17 in

The highly social acorn woodpecker lives in cohesive family groups of up to 16 birds, which commonly stay together year-round to protect communal food stores (mainly acorns stored in hole-studded "granary trees") and nesting sites. During the breeding season, only 1 or 2 pairs will actually mate and produce eggs, which are laid in a single large nest cavity. Non-breeding members of the group help incubate the eggs and raise the young. **Where found:** oak forests, riparian woodlands and parks; throughout most of wooded California year-round.

Nuttall's Woodpecker

Picoides nuttallii

Length: 7–7½ in
Wingspan: 13½ in

Probing in crevices and flaking off bark in search of wood-boring insects, insect eggs and ants, Nuttall's woodpecker hops acrobatically on the undersides of branches and deftly scales tree trunks. • Thomas Nuttall traveled across the country writing about natural history; his many contributions to ornithology include his *Manual of Ornithology of the United States and Canada*. **Where found:** permanent resident in foothills, valley bottoms and woodlands, particularly oak; throughout much of the interior and near the coast year-round.

Northern Flicker

Colaptes auratus

Length: 12–13 in
Wingspan: 20 in

With robin-like hops, the northern flicker scours the ground of grassy meadows and forest clearings in search of invertebrates, particularly ants that it squashes and preens itself with for the formic acid, which kills small parasites on its skin and feathers. The flicker will also bathe in dusty depressions—the dust particles absorb oils and bacteria that can harm the bird's feathers. • The least arboreal of our woodpeckers, this species spends more time on the ground than other woodpeckers; while nesting in tree cavities, it behaves in a more characteristic manner—clinging, rattling and drumming on tree trunks. **Where found**: most broken or open forests, woodlands, forest edges, fields and meadows, riparian woodlands and suburban parks and gardens to an elevation of 10,000 ft; occasional visitor to backyard bird feeders; throughout most of wooded California year-round.

Black Phoebe

Sayornis nigricans

Length: 6½–7 in
Wingspan: 10½–11 in

With delicate sallies from perch to ground, this phoebe is able
to capture just about any insect that zips past its perch. The
black phoebe sometimes catches prey on the water's surface,
perching on high rocks when tree limbs are unavailable,
and may even catch small fish on occasion. **Where found:**
resident near water in semi-open habitats, typically from sea level
to 4000 ft, including riparian woodlands, steep-walled canyons,
cities and farmlands with wet areas; widespread year-round.

Pacific-slope Flycatcher

Empidonax difficilis

Length: 5 in
Wingspan: 8 in

Flycatchers are hard to distinguish from each other, and it wasn't
until late in the 20th century that the Pacific-slope flycatcher was
recognized as its own species. Nevertheless, it is a common
songbird in our area, and its song is more distinctive than its
looks. The upslurred *suweeet* call is a familiar sound in any
moist woodland in spring. • This flycatcher sits perched on
exposed branches, waiting for potential prey to fly past; when it spots a target, this
quick flycatcher lives up to its name, snatching insects in flight and then returning
to its perch to await the next tasty passerby. **Where found:** moist hardwood or
mixed forests; in foothills and valleys of the western cismontane in summer.

Western Kingbird

Tyrannus verticalis

Length: 8–9 in
Wingspan: 15½ in

Kingbirds are a group of flycatchers that perch on wires,
power lines or fence posts in open habitats in search of insect
prey and fearlessly chase out larger birds from their breeding
territories. Once you have witnessed a kingbird's brave
attacks against much larger birds, such as crows and hawks,
you'll understand why this rabble-rouser was awarded its
regal common name. • The tumbling aerial courtship display of the western kingbird
is an entertaining spring scene in Southern California. The male twists and turns
as he rises to heights of 65 ft above the ground, stalls, then tumbles and flips his
way back to the earth. **Where found:** any open habitat, such as irrigated valleys,
open or riparian woodlands and woodland edges; widespread summer resident.

Warbling Vireo

Vireo gilvus

Length: 5–5½ in
Wingspan: 8–9 in

The charming warbling vireo is a common spring and summer resident, often settling close to urban areas; its velvety voice (with a warbling quality not heard in other vireos) may be heard in local parks, backyards and farmlands. Because the warbling vireo lacks any splashy field marks, it is undetectable unless it moves from one leaf-hidden stage to another. It nests in a horizontal fork of a tree or shrub, making a hanging basket-like cup nest of grass, roots, plant down and spider's silk. The pair incubates 4 eggs for 12 days. **Where found:** *Breeding:* riparian wooded areas, open bigleaf maple forests and mixed forests. *In migration:* almost any woodland but prefers hardwood stands and residential areas; throughout most of wooded California in summer.

Western Scrub-Jay

Aphelocoma californica

Length: 11½ in
Wingspan: 16 in

This intelligent corvid harvests fallen acorns and stores them in holes that it has dug into the ground with its strong bill; it uses a rock or concrete slab as a type of anvil to crack the acorns open. Any acorns the western scrub-jay does not eat have been effectively planted, and many germinate and regenerate the oak stands. **Where found:** chaparral and dry, brushy, open areas of oak and pinyon-juniper woodlands, mixed oak-conifer forests and riparian woodlands; also found in suburban parks and gardens; common and widespread year-round resident.

American Crow

Corvus brachyrhynchos

Length: 17–21 in
Wingspan: 36 in

The noise that most often emanates from these treetop squawkers seems unrepresentative of their intelligence. Crows often drop walnuts or clams from great heights onto a hard surface to crack the shells. These wary, clever birds are also impressive mimics, able to whine like a dog and laugh or cry like a human. • Crows are family oriented, and the young from the previous year may help their parents raise the nestlings. **Where found:** urban areas, agricultural fields and other open areas with scattered woodlands; widespread year-round.

Common Raven

Corvus corax

Length: 21–23 in
Wingspan: 4 ft

The common raven soars with a wingspan comparable to that of a hawk, traveling along coastlines, over deserts, along mountain ridges and even over the arctic tundra. Few birds occupy such a large natural range. • From producing complex vocalizations to playfully sliding down snowbanks, this raucous bird exhibits behaviors that many people once thought of as exclusively human. Glorified in Native American culture, the raven seems to demonstrate an apparent enjoyment of life. **Where found:** coniferous and mixed forests and woodlands, townsites, campgrounds and landfills; widespread year-round.

Horned Lark

Eremophila alpestris

Length: 7 in
Wingspan: 12 in

One way to distinguish the horned lark from a sparrow is by its method of locomotion: horned larks walk, but sparrows hop. • This bird's dark tail contrasts with its light brown body and belly, and it has 2 unique black "horns." Look for this feature to spot the horned lark in its open-country habitat. • In spring, the male performs an impressive, high-speed, plummeting courtship dive. **Where found:** treeless, open country, especially barren-ground and short-grass habitats; from sea level to over 12,000 ft; widespread year-round.

Tree Swallow

Tachycineta bicolor

Length: 5½ in
Wingspan: 14½ in

Tree swallows are often the first migrants to appear in our area in spring and can be seen perched beside their fence-post nest boxes. When conditions are favorable, these busy birds are known to return to their young 10 to 20 times per hour (about 140 to 300 times a day!). • In the evening and during light rains, small groups of foraging tree swallows sail gracefully above rivers and wetlands, catching stoneflies, mayflies and caddisflies. **Where found:** open areas, fencelines with bluebird nest boxes and fringes of open woodlands, especially near water; widespread but tends to be more western in range in winter and interior and northern in range in summer.

Cliff Swallow

Petrochelidon pyrrhonota

Length: 5½ in
Wingspan: 13½ in

Cliff swallows, the most widespread swallow in Southern California, nest on various human-made structures. Entire colonies under bridges can be wiped out during floods. Master mud masons, cliff swallows roll mud into balls with their bills and press the pellets together to form their characteristic gourd-shaped nests. • The similar barn swallow (*Hirundo rustica*) also builds mud nests but typically on barns and other buildings; it can be identified in flight by its long forked tail. **Where found:** *Breeding:* cliffs, rimrocks, bridges, buildings, tunnels and dams from sea level to 9000 ft. *In migration:* open lowland areas including meadows, farmlands, golf courses, beaches, rivers and marshes; widespread summer resident.

Oak Titmouse

Baeolophus inornatus

Length: 5–5½ in
Wingspan: 7½ in

The nasal *tsick-a-dee-dee* call of the oak
titmouse is a characteristic sound of the
sprawling oak woodlands of interior California.
• The oak titmouse nests in natural cavities, rotted stumps
and occasionally in abandoned woodpecker nests. The female fills the
cavity with vegetation, feathers and hair and incubates her 6–8 eggs for about
2 weeks. The parents mate for life, and both feed the young. **Where found:** year-
round in mixed oak and riparian woodlands; widespread throughout the western
cismontane wherever there are oak trees but absent from high elevations.

Wrentit

Chamaea fasciata

Length: 6–6½ in
Wingspan: 7 in

Unlike most songbirds, wrentits do not migrate, and they
mate for life. They are secretive birds, preferring to remain
concealed within dense tangles of brush and scrub and
rarely crossing open areas where predators could interrupt
their feeble flights without warning. A pair of wrentits may spend an entire lifetime
together in an area no larger than a few acres. **Where found:** hilly brushlands,
lowland and montane chaparral, coastal sage scrub, northern coastal scrub and
shrubby tangles along the edges of streams and suburban gardens; readily colonizes regenerating logged sites; year-round throughout most of the southwest.

Bushtit

Psaltriparus minimus

Length: 4–4½ in
Wingspan: 6 in

Bushtits catch your eye as they endlessly bounce from one
shrubby perch to another and catch your ear with charming,
bell-like, tinkling calls. Hyperactive in everything they do,
these tiny, fluffy, gregarious birds are constantly on the move, either fastidiously
building a nest or roaming about in post-breeding bands of up to 40 members.
When nest building, they neurotically test every fiber to ensure its suitability.
• Bushtits will desert both nest and mate if intruded upon. **Where found:** year-
round resident of juniper and oak forests, riparian brushlands, chaparral and
large, residential gardens in southwestern California; widespread year-round.

Pygmy Nuthatch

Sitta pygmaea

Length: 4–4½ in
Wingspan: 8 in

You will notice a nuthatch immediately, if not by its attractive coloring than by its manner of moving down the trunk of a tree head first as it searches for seeds and invertebrates. This technique allows it to find food that upward-moving woodpeckers miss. The pygmy nuthatch is also noticeably energetic, noisy and gregarious, appearing in small flocks that increase in size in fall and winter; in winter, the flock will communally roost in a tree cavity. **Where found:** pine and pine-fir forests, from sea level along the coast to 9000 ft; widespread year-round in most of wooded Southern California.

Bewick's Wren

Thryomanes bewickii

Length: 5–5½ in
Wingspan: 7 in

This charming wren scans its surroundings with endless curiosity and exuberant animation as its long, narrow tail flits and waves from side to side. It is always on the lookout for insects to prey upon or intruders to angrily scold. **Where found:** lower and middle elevations in dense vines and shrubby tangles bordering woodlands and shrublands within pinyon-juniper and oak woodlands, chaparral, riparian thickets, parks, gardens and brush piles; widespread year-round resident.

Ruby-crowned Kinglet

Regulus calendula

Length: 4 in
Wingspan: 7½ in

This kinglet's familiar voice echoes through our boreal forest in spring and summer. Not only does the male ruby-crowned kinglet possess a loud, complex, warbling song to draw attention to himself, he also has a nifty red "mohawk" to help attract a mate and defend his territory in spring. Unfortunately, his distinctive crown is only visible during the breeding season, leaving him with just his dull, olive green plumage for the rest of the year. **Where found:** *Breeding:* subalpine coniferous forests at 4000–10,000 ft. *In migration* and *winter:* practically all trees and shrubbery throughout Southern California; may be observed year-round in the northern limits of the region.

Blue-gray Gnatcatcher

Polioptila caerulea

Length: 4½ in
Wingspan: 6 in

The fidgety blue-gray gnatcatcher is constantly on
the move. This woodland inhabitant holds its tail upward
like a wren and issues a quiet, banjo-like *twang* while flitting rest-
lessly from shrub to shrub. • Gnatcatcher pairs remain close once a
bond is established, and both parents share the responsibilities of nest
building, incubation and raising the young. Like most songbirds,
blue-gray gnatcatchers mature quickly and fly as far as South America within
months of hatching. **Where found:** deciduous woodlands along streams, ponds,
lakes and swamps; also in orchards, shrubby tangles along woodland edges and
oak savannas; widespread throughout most of wooded California year-round.

Western Bluebird

Sialia mexicana

Length: 7 in
Wingspan: 13½ in

Like the feathers of all bluebirds, western bluebird
feathers are not actually pigmented blue. The color
is a result of the feathers' microscopic structure,
which produces various hues of blue by irides-
cence or by the Tyndall effect, which is the same
process that causes the sky to appear blue. • Western bluebirds usually succeed in raising 2 broods
per year, producing the second clutch of eggs as soon
as the first brood leaves the nest. **Where found:** broken oak and oak-conifer
woodlands, oak savannahs, riparian woodlands and open pine forests near sea
level to 7000 ft; widespread year-round but populations along the eastern portion
of the state are typically observed only in winter.

Hermit Thrush

Catharus guttatus

Length: 7 in
Wingspan: 11½ in

The hermit thrush's haunting, flute-like song may be
one of the most beautiful natural melodies, and it is
almost always preceded with a single questioning
note. • This thrush feeds mainly on insects, worms and snails during
summer, but it adds a wide variety of fruit to its winter diet. **Where found:** well-
shaded coniferous and high evergreen-oak forests, ridges on upper hillsides and
montane riparian areas near sea level to 10,000 ft; widespread winter resident.

American Robin

Turdus migratorius

Length: 10 in
Wingspan: 17 in

The American robin is a familiar and common sight on lawns as it searches for worms. In winter, its diet switches to fruit, which can attract flocks to fruit trees to feed. • American robins build cup-shaped nests of grass, moss and mud. The female incubates 4 light blue eggs and raises up to 3 broods per year. The male cares for the fledglings from the first brood while the female incubates the second clutch of eggs. **Where found:** riparian woodlands, forests with open meadows and forest edges; widespread throughout most of wooded California year-round.

Northern Mockingbird

Mimus polyglottos

Length: 10 in
Wingspan: 14 in

The northern mockingbird has an amazing vocal repertoire that includes more than 400 different song types, which it belts out incessantly throughout the breeding season, serenading into the night during a full moon. The mockingbird can imitate almost anything. In some instances, it replicates notes so accurately that even computerized sound analysis may be unable to detect the difference between the original source and the mockingbird's imitation. The scientific name *polyglottos* is Greek for "many tongues" and refers to this bird's ability to mimic a wide variety of sounds. **Where found:** hedges, suburban gardens and orchard margins with an abundance of available fruit; widespread year-round.

European Starling

Sturnus vulgaris

Length: 8½ in
Wingspan: 16 in

The European starling spread across North America after being released in New York City's Central Park in 1890 and 1891. It was brought to New York as part of the local Shakespeare society's plan to introduce all the birds mentioned in their favorite author's writings. • This highly adaptable bird not only takes over the nest sites of native cavity nesters, such as woodpeckers, but it also mimics the sounds of killdeers, red-tailed hawks, soras and meadowlarks. **Where found:** cities, towns, residential areas, farmyards, pastures, feedlots, woodland fringes and clearings; widespread year-round.

Cedar Waxwing

Bombycilla cedrorum

Length: 7 in
Wingspan: 12 in

With its black mask and slick hairdo, the cedar waxwing has a heroic look. To court a mate, the gentlemanly male hops toward a female and offers her a berry. The female accepts the berry and hops away, then stops and hops back toward the male to offer him the berry in return. **Where found:** wherever ripe berries are available, including residential areas, hardwood and mixed forests, woodland edges, fruit orchards, young pine plantations and riparian hardwoods among conifers; widespread throughout most of wooded Southern California in winter.

Orange-crowned Warbler

Vermivora celata

Length: 5 in
Wingspan: 7 in

The nondescript orange-crowned warbler causes identification problems for many birders. Its drab, olive yellow appearance and lack of field marks make it frustratingly similar to females of other warbler species, and the male's orange crown patch is seldom visible. • This small warbler is usually seen gleaning insects from the leaves and buds of low shrubs, and it routinely feeds on sap or insects attracted to the sap wells drilled by other birds. **Where found:** any wooded habitat and area with tall shrubs; typically western cismontane to the coast year-round.

Yellow Warbler

Dendroica petechia

Length: 5 in
Wingspan: 8 in

The yellow warbler is often parasitized by the brown-headed cowbird and can recognize cowbird eggs, but rather than tossing them out, this warbler will build another nest overtop the old eggs or abandon the nest site completely. • The widely distributed yellow warbler arrives in May, flitting from branch to branch in search of juicy caterpillars, aphids and beetles and singing its *sweet-sweet-sweet summer sweet* song. It is often mistakenly called the "wild canary." **Where found:** moist, open woodlands, dense scrub, scrubby meadows, second-growth woodlands, riparian woods and urban parks and gardens; widespread summer resident.

Yellow-rumped Warbler

Dendroica coronata

Length: 5½ in
Wingspan: 9–9½ in

Yellow-rumped warblers are the most abundant and widespread wood-warblers in North America as well as one of the most attractive. Eucalyptus and trees laden with fruit attract these birds to coastal cities in winter, but in summer they retreat to cooler temperatures in the mountains. • This species has 2 forms: the yellow-throated "Audubon's warbler" of the west, and the white-throated "myrtle warbler," which breeds in the north and east of the Rockies. **Where found:** hardwood and mixed thickets and woodlands; along the coast and in interior valleys; widespread in winter but observed year-round only in northern low elevations and coastal extents of its Southern Californian range.

Townsend's Warbler

Dendroica townsendi

Length: 5 in
Wingspan: 8 in

Choosing to nest at the tops of conifer trees in mountain forests, this warbler may be hard to spot outside of winter. During winter, it can be seen with other hardy birds in the dense foliage along the coast or in residential gardens, where it is attracted to suet feeders. With an omnivorous appetite, the Townsend's warbler gleans vegetation and eats seeds and plant galls but also hawks for insects. **Where found:** coniferous and mixed woods, urban parks and coastal thickets in winter.

Common Yellowthroat

Geothlypis trichas

Length: 5 in
Wingspan: 7 in

The bumblebee colors of the male common yellow-throat's black mask and yellow throat identify this skulking wetland resident. The male sings his *witchety-witchety-witchety* song from strategically chosen cattail perches that he visits in rotation, fiercely guarding his territory against the intrusion of other males. • Many wetland species have been displaced in California because of urban and agricultural development, and the common yellowthroat is no exception. **Where found:** cattail marshes, sedge wetlands, riparian areas, beaver ponds and wet, overgrown meadows or vegetation surrounding freshwater bodies; widespread year-round except in the northeastern limits of Southern California, where it is observed mostly in summer.

Wilson's Warbler

Wilsonia pusilla

Length: 4½–5 in
Wingspan: 7 in

The petite Wilson's warbler darts energetically through the undergrowth in its tireless search for insects. Fueled by its energy-rich prey, this indefatigable bird seems to behave as if a motionless moment would break some unwritten law of warblerdom. • This bird is named for ornithologist Alexander Wilson, who pioneered studies of North American birds. **Where found:** *Breeding:* in dense deciduous shrub cover, especially willow and alder. *Nonbreeding:* shrubby, wetland-riparian habitats, wet mountain meadows and edges of small lakes and springs; summer resident in western cismontane, though not common in the far south of the state.

Western Tanager

Piranga ludoviciana

Length: 7 in
Wingspan: 11–11½ in

The western tanager brings with it the colors of a tropical visitor on its summer vacation in our area. This bird raises a new generation of young and takes advantage of the seasonal explosion of food in our forests before heading back to its exotic wintering grounds in Mexico and Central America. • The male western tanager spends long periods of time singing from the same perch, sounding somewhat like a robin with a sore throat. **Where found:** mature coniferous and mixed forests, especially ponderosa pine, and fruit-bearing trees and shrubs in riparian woodlands; summer resident in western cismontane.

California Towhee

Pipilo crissalis

Length: 8½–10 in
Wingspan: 12 in

California towhees are highly territorial and proclaim their territory by singing out with a sharp, metallic *chink*. They are so territorial that male towhees have been observed attacking their own reflections in low-mounted windows. Yet, they are very accepting of their human neighbors and are commonly seen foraging under picnic tables, on patios or at the feet of admiring birders. **Where found:** broken chaparral and shrubby tangles, thickets and hedgerows near streams, gardens, parks, farmyards and woodlands; year-round resident of the western cismontane.

Savannah Sparrow

Passerculus sandwichensis

Length: 5–6½ in
Wingspan: 8½–9 in

Like most sparrows, the savannah sparrow generally prefers to stay out of sight, though small flocks and individuals are sometimes seen darting across roads, fields or beaches. It is not apt to fly even if threatened, preferring to run swiftly and inconspicuously through tall grasses as an escape tactic. **Where found:** coastal grasslands, estuary meadows, salt marshes along the coastline, grassy interior valleys and borders of mountain streams, agricultural fields and alkaline lakeshores; widespread winter resident.

Song Sparrow

Melospiza melodia

Length: 6–7 in
Wingspan: 8 in

Although its plumage is unremarkable, the well-named song sparrow is among the great singers of the bird world. By the time a male song sparrow is only a few months old, he has already created a courtship tune of his own, having learned the basics of melody and rhythm from his father and rival males. A well-stocked backyard feeder may be a fair trade for a sweet song, especially near the end of winter—the most common lyric this bird seems to sing is *hip-hip-hooray boys, the spring is here again*. **Where found:** hardwood brush in forests and open country, near water or in lush vegetation in chaparral, riparian willows, marshy habitats and residential areas; widespread year-round resident.

White-crowned Sparrow

Zonotrichia leucophrys

Length: 5½–7 in
Wingspan: 9½ in

In winter, large, bold and smartly patterned white-crowned sparrows brighten brushy hedgerows, overgrown fields and riparian areas. During cold weather, these sparrows may visit bird feeders stocked with cracked corn. • Several different races of white-crowned sparrow occur in North America, all with similar plumage but different song dialects. Research into this sparrow has given science tremendous insight into bird physiology, homing behavior and the geographic variability of song dialects. **Where found:** areas with a mix of shrub or tree cover and open ground; in mixed flocks in residential areas, parks, gardens and unplowed croplands; widespread winter resident.

Dark-eyed Junco

Junco hyemalis

Length: 6–7 in
Wingspan: 9 in

Juncos usually congregate in backyards with bird feeders and sheltering conifers—with such amenities at their disposal, more and more juncos are appearing in urban areas. These birds spend most of their time on the ground, snatching up seeds underneath bird feeders, and they are readily flushed from wooded trails. • There are 5 closely related dark-eyed junco subspecies in North America that share similar habits but differ in coloration and range. **Where found:** in shrubby woodland borders and backyard feeders; widespread winter resident.

Black-headed Grosbeak

Pheucticus melanocephalus

Length: 7–8½ in
Wingspan: 12½ in

Black-headed grosbeaks will quickly make your acquaintance on almost any spring or summer hike in the woods. These birds are marvelous singers, advertising breeding territories with extended bouts of complex, accented caroling. Males sing from slightly sheltered perches near the top of a tree, while females forage and conduct nesting chores within the cover of interior foliage. **Where found:** hardwood and mixed forests, bottomland willows and cottonwoods, riparian and lakeshore woodlands, rich oak woodlands and high-elevation aspen groves; summer resident throughout wooded areas of Southern California.

115

Red-winged Blackbird

Agelaius phoeniceus

Length: 7½–9 in
Wingspan: 13 in

The male red-winged blackbird wears his bright red shoulders like armor—together with his short, raspy song, they are key in defending his territory from rivals. • Nearly every cattail marsh worthy of note in our region hosts red-winged blackbirds and resonates with that proud, distinctive song. The female's cryptic coloration allows her to sit inconspicuously on her nest, blending in perfectly among the cattails or shoreline bushes. **Where found:** cattail marshes, wet meadows and ditches, croplands and shoreline shrubs throughout Southern California year-round.

Western Meadowlark

Sturnella neglecta

Length: 9–9½ in
Wingspan: 14½ in

In the early 19th century, members of the Lewis and Clark expedition overlooked the western meadowlark, mistaking it for the very similar looking eastern meadowlark, hence the scientific name *neglecta*. • A breeding pair bond is established with an elaborate courtship dance; the male and female face each other, raise their bills high in the air and perform a grassland ballet. • The western meadowlark has benefited from land management that protects grasslands from overgrazing or agriculture. **Where found:** grassy meadows, native prairie and pastures, croplands, weedy fields and grassy roadsides; widespread year-round.

Brewer's Blackbird

Euphagus cyanocephalus

Length: 8–10 in
Wingspan: 15–15½ in

Urban and agricultural development has been very beneficial to Brewer's blackbird. Agriculture and ranching provide ample forage opportunities, and landscaped trees and tall shrubs offer sheltered nesting sites. This bird has also found a niche opportunistically feeding on road-killed insects. **Where found:** wet meadows, grasslands, shores, roadsides, landfills, golf courses, urban and suburban parks and gardens, ranches, farmyards, pastures and freshwater marshes from sea level to nearly 9000 ft; widespread year-round.

Brown-headed Cowbird

Molothrus ater

Length: 6–8 in
Wingspan: 12 in

These nomads historically followed bison herds across the Great Plains (they now follow cattle), so they never stayed in one area long enough to build and tend a nest. Instead, brown-headed cowbirds lay their eggs in the nests of other birds and have become the most successful brood parasites in North America. **Where found:** agricultural and residential areas, fields, woodland edges, utility cutlines, roadsides, fencelines, landfills, campgrounds and areas near cattle; widespread year-round.

Bullock's Oriole

Icterus bullockii

Length: 9 in
Wingspan: 12 in

Although Bullock's orioles commonly nest in deciduous woodlands and even suburban areas from mid-March to mid-August, most people are unaware of them. The male's colorful plumage blends remarkably well with the dappled light of the bird's upper-canopy summer home. Finding the drab olive, gray and white female is even more difficult. • The orioles' elaborate hanging nests become easily visible when the cottonwoods lose their leaves in fall. **Where found:** riparian woodlands with large cottonwoods, willows and sycamores; oak canyons and oak woodlands; suburban parks and gardens, isolated tree groves and shelter-belts in farmyards; widespread summer resident; year-round in San Diego and Orange Counties.

House Finch

Carpodacus mexicanus

Length: 5–6 in
Wingspan: 9½ in

Formerly restricted to the arid Southwest and Mexico, the house finch is now commonly found through-out the continental U.S. and has even been introduced to Hawaii. Only the resourceful house finch has been aggressive and stubborn enough to successfully outcompete the house sparrow. • The male house finch's plumage varies in color from light yellow to bright red, but females will choose to breed with the reddest males. **Where found:** open fields and woodlands, backyard feeders and disturbed areas, including farms, ranches and towns; widespread year-round.

American Goldfinch

Carduelis tristis

Length: 4½–5 in
Wingspan: 9 in

Like vibrant rays of sunshine, American gold-finches cheerily flutter over weedy fields, gardens and along roadsides, perching on late-summer thistle heads or poking through dandelion patches in search of seeds. It is hard to miss their jubilant *po-ta-to-chip* call and distinctive, undulating flight style. • Because these acrobatic birds regularly feed while hanging upside down, finch feeders are designed with the seed openings below the perches. **Where found:** weedy fields, chaparral, woodland edges, meadows, riparian areas, parks and gardens; widespread year-round resident but may be in the eastern ranges only in winter. **Also known as:** willow goldfinch.

Lazuli Bunting

Passerina amoena

Length: 5½ in
Wingspan: 8¾ in

This bird is named for the male's striking blue plumage, which is the color of the gemstone lapis lazuli. • Males set up territorial districts in which neighboring males copy and learn their songs from one another, producing "song territories." Each male within a song territory sings a variation of *swip-swip-swip zu zu ee, see see sip see see* with slight differences in the series of wiry, piercing notes and syllables, producing his own acoustic fingerprint. • Lazuli buntings are widespread throughout our area during summer before undergoing a partial molt and then migrating south in August to the American Southwest and northwestern Mexico. **Where found:** willow and alder shrublands, open brushy areas, forest edges, riparian thickets, young burns and hedges; widespread summer resident.

House Sparrow

Passer domesticus

Length: 5½–6½ in
Wingspan: 9½ in

This abundant and conspicuous bird was introduced to North America in the 1850s as part of a plan to control the insects that were damaging grain and cereal crops. As it turns out, these birds are largely vegetarian! • The house sparrow will usurp territory and nests of other native birds, such as bluebirds, cliff swallows or purple martins, and has a high reproductive output of 4 clutches per year, with up to 8 young per clutch. **Where found:** townsites, urban and suburban areas, farmyards and agricultural areas, railway yards and other developed areas; widespread year-round.

AMPHIBIANS & REPTILES

Amphibians and reptiles are commonly referred to as cold-blooded, but this term is misleading. Although these animals lack the ability to generate internal body heat, they are not necessarily cold-blooded. They are ectothermic or poikilothermic, meaning that the temperature of the surrounding environment governs their body temperature. The animal will obtain heat from sunlight, warm rocks and logs, and warmed earth. Reptiles and amphibians hibernate in winter in cold areas, and some reptiles estivate in summer in hot regions. Both amphibians and reptiles molt as they grow to larger body sizes.

Amphibians (newts, salamanders, frogs and toads) are smooth-skinned and most live in moist habitats. They typically lay shell-less eggs in jelly-like masses in water. These eggs hatch into gilled larvae (e.g., tadpoles), which then metamorphose into adults with lungs and legs. Amphibians can regenerate their skin and often even entire limbs. Male and female amphibians often differ in size and color, and males may have other diagnostic features when sexually mature, such as the vocal sacs in many frogs and toads.

Reptiles are fully terrestrial vertebrates with scaly skin. In this guide, the representatives are skinks, lizards, turtles and snakes. Most lay eggs and bury them in loose soil, but some snakes and lizards give birth to live young. Reptiles do not have a larval stage.

Newts & Salamanders
p. 120

Frogs & Toads
pp. 121–22

Turtles
p. 123

Lizards
pp. 124–25

Snakes
pp. 126–27

California Newt

Taricha torosa

Length: 5–8 in

The California newt lives a dual lifestyle as a terrestrial, nonbreeding eft before becoming an aquatic newt. As a terrestrial eft in late summer and fall, it hides under logs and in rock crevices; then at the first rains of winter, it migrates to the water and, upon entering, transforms into an aquatic newt and breeds. • It announces its toxicity to predators by showing off its bright orange underbelly, which it displays by arching its back, raising its head and pointing its tail and legs upward. **Where found:** moist forests from sea level to above 6000 ft; along the coast and Coast Range to San Diego County, with a disjunct population in the southern Sierra Nevadas from northern Kern County northward.

California Tiger Salamander

Ambystoma californiense

Length: 6–8½ in

The increasingly rare California tiger salamander has been extirpated from more than half of its original range, and its current range is fragmented by agricultural development. It easily hybridizes with the non-native tiger salamander (*A. tigrinum*). • This fossorial species spends most of its time underground, emerging during the fall rains in mass migrations to breeding ponds. **Where found:** grasslands, oak savannahs, edges of mixed woodlands and low-elevation coniferous forests; along the coast south to Santa Barbara.

Western Spadefoot

Spea hammondii

Length: 1½–2½ in

Named for the dark, wedge-shaped "spade" found near the heel of their hind feet, these toads burrow underground during the day and resurface at night to hunt for insects. A small hump between their eyes, called a boss, protects their heads as they push their way through the soil to the surface. • These relatively smooth-skinned amphibians are not true toads because they lack parotid glands and warts; instead, they have small, lumpy, black and red tubercles on olive green to grayish green skin. **Where found**: arid regions from sea level to 4000 ft along the West Coast to Baja California.

Western Toad

Bufo boreas

Length: 2–5 in

Touching a toad will not give you warts, but the western toad does have a way of discouraging unwanted affection. When handled, it secretes a toxin from large parotid glands behind its eyes that irritates the mouth of potential predators. • This large, gray, green or brown toad is a voracious predator of insects and other tasty invertebrates such as worms and slugs. • The arroyo toad *(B. californicus)* is also found in southwestern California; it is similar in appearance to its western cousin but is smaller (2–3½ in) and lacks the light-colored stripe down its back that *B. boreas* sports. **Where found:** near springs, streams, meadows and woodlands from north-central California southward, east of the deserts, into Baja California.

Bullfrog

Rana catesbeiana

Length: up to 8 in

Bullfrogs are not native to California but were introduced in the early 1900s. They are very large and live an average of 7–9 years, with records of captive individuals living 16 years. • Bullfrogs are predatory, eating anything they can swallow, including certain snakes and fish, and are incredibly prolific, making them a significant threat to native frog populations. **Where found:** warm, still, shallow, vegetated waters of lakes, ponds, rivers and bogs; throughout most of southern California but absent from dry deserts and high elevations.

121

Red-legged Frog

Rana draytonii

Length: 1¾–5¼ in

Once hunted for its legs, prized for culinary purposes, this frog is now heavily preyed upon by bullfrogs. However, habitat loss and water pollution are the red-legged frog's greatest threats. Sightings of this threatened native frog should be reported to the U.S. Fish and Wildlife Service. • The frog caught in a swamp near Angels Camp in Mark Twain's "The Notorious Jumping Frog of Calaveras County" was probably a red-legged frog. **Where found:** deep, still or slow-moving ponds or intermittent streams with emergent riparian vegetation; ranges along the coast and up into the foothills from Northern California to northern Baja California.

Pacific Treefrog

Hyla regilla

Length: ¾–2 in

Pacific treefrogs have adhesive toe pads that enable them to climb vertical surfaces and cling to the tiniest branch. The frogs can also change color within a few minutes, allowing them to blend into their immediate surroundings. Colors include green, brown, gray, tan, reddish and black; dark spots are often present. • Despite their name, these frogs are often terrestrial, choosing moist, grassy habitats. **Where found:** riparian areas and low-elevation shrubby areas close to water; throughout southwestern California and the Channel Islands. **Also known as:** *Pseudacris regilla.*

Western Painted Turtle

Chrysemys picta

Length: 4–10 in

This colorful turtle has a mainly vegetarian diet, which is supplemented with invertebrates, amphibian larvae and small fish. • The western painted turtle is the most widespread species of turtle in North America but is not native to California and is suspected of competing with the native western pond turtle. Another introduced turtle is the red-eared slider *(Trachemys scripta),* which is farmed worldwide for the pet industry (and often subsequently escapes into the wild) and in Asia for food; it has a green shell and large red marking on the side of its head. **Where found:** shallow, muddy-bottomed waterbodies with abundant plant growth, such as sloughs, ponds, lakes and marshes, and open banks along sluggish rivers with oxbows; throughout coastal Southern California.

Western Pond Turtle

Actinemys marmorata

Length: 4–9 in

Unless they see you first and quickly disappear into the water, western pond turtles are typically seen either singly or in groups, basking in the sun on a rock or log in a pond. • Pond turtles feed mainly on crayfish, insects, amphibian eggs and larvae and aquatic plants. Raccoons, large fish and bullfrogs prey on pond turtle eggs and juveniles, but once the turtles mature, predation rates drop significantly. These turtles can live more than 50 years in the wild. **Where found:** mud-bottomed ponds, lakes, ditches, sloughs, marshes and slow-moving streams; throughout coastal Southern California and along the Coast Range. **Also known as:** mud turtle; formerly called *Clemmys marmorata.*

Desert Tortoise

Gopherus agassizii

Length: 14 in

The desert tortoise, an icon of desert wildlife, can live more than a 100 years. This shy tortoise has quietly and gently endured many threats to its dwindling popula-tion, including illegal collection, harassment, disease, road kill, depredation and loss of habitat. The species was given federal protection in 1990 as a threatened species, and the establishment of protected areas such as Joshua Tree National Park is improving its chances for survival. The desert tortoise is vegetarian, lives in deep (to 15 ft) burrows and lays clutches of 1–12 eggs, from which sand-dollar-sized hatchlings emerge between July and October. **Where found:** throughout the Mojave Desert, east of the Salton Basin.

Southern Alligator Lizard

Elgaria multicarinata

Length: 12 in

Think twice before picking up a southern alligator lizard because it is notorious for biting and, perhaps even worse, defecating foul-smelling feces. • This small lizard preys upon pretty much anything smaller than itself, which includes insects and spiders, scorpions, snails, slugs, worms, smaller lizards, baby mice, birds and bird eggs. **Where found:** pine and mixed oak-pine and brushy chaparral, oak woodlands and savannahs of the western foothills; west of the Transverse and Peninsular ranges from San Diego County northward, in the Mojave Desert along the Mojave River and on Santa Catalina and San Nicolas islands.

Sagebrush Lizard

Sceloporus graciosus

Length: 1½–5½ in

Sagebrush lizards hunt insects, spiders, mites and ticks on the ground or in shrubs. They bask on sun-warmed rocks or hide in shady bushes to maintain their body temperature; studies report lizards allowing themselves to overheat in the hot sun to induce a form of fever to break bacterial infections. • Males have blue belly patches and mottling on the throat; the pink sides and neck become brighter on females during the breeding season. Sagebrush lizards do not have the large, pointed dorsal scales typical of *Sceloporus* species. **Where found:** chaparral, montane habitats and dry areas with sagebrush; within the Transverse and Peninsular ranges.

Western Fence Lizard

Sceloporus occidentalis

Length: 7 in

The western fence lizard's diagnostic characteristics include bright blue patches on the sides of the abdomen and under the throat (though on the female, this coloring can be faded or absent) as well as prickly looking scales on the back. The males flaunt their bright blue bellies during breeding season to impress females and challenge rival males. **Where found:** open, sunny areas with logs, fence posts or rocks to bask on; valleys, mountains, oak woodlands and coastal areas west of the Sierras; coastal and montane areas from San Diego County northward and the Great Basin Desert; mostly absent (isolated pockets at high elevations) from the southern deserts. **Also known as:** blue-bellied lizard.

Western Whiptail

Aspidoscelis tigris

Length: 13 in

Mostly tail, with a body length of only 2½–4½ in, the western whiptail adds on significantly more length by sticking out its impressively long forked tongue. • For food, it digs for buried insects, spiders, scorpions and occasionally other lizards. • A juvenile western whiptail has a pale blue to bluish gray tail, which often leads to it being mistaken for a western skink. **Where found:** oak and chaparral regions, arid flats and hillsides of sagebrush or other shrubby areas; throughout Southern California, but eastern and western populations are divided into separate subspecies. **Also known as:** tiger whiptail; formerly belonged to the *Cnemidophorus* genus.

Western Skink

Eumeces skiltonianus

Length: 7½ in

The juvenile western skink sports a bright blue tail that, when grabbed by predators, easily breaks off and continues to writhe while the skink makes its escape; the skink will soon grow a new tail. An adult's tail fades to become reddish orange during the breeding season. • The western skink feeds on insects and spiders. **Where found:** among leaf litter and underneath bark and rocks; burrows in grasslands, woodlands, pine forests, sagebrush and chaparral; rocky areas near streams with plenty of vegetation; most common in upland habitat and mesa tops; throughout southwestern California and on Santa Catalina island, but absent from the southern deserts. **Also known as:** Skilton's skink; *Plestiodon skiltonianus*.

Yellow-bellied Racer

Coluber constrictor

Length: 2–7 ft; typically under 3 ft

The racer relies on speed to catch prey and escape danger. On the ground, it moves with its head held high for a better view of the terrain; it will also climb shrubs to find birds and insects. • Certain individuals have a bluish cast to the body. **Where found:** open forests, wooded hills, grassy ditches, riparian areas, open juniper and pine forests, rocky canyons, sagebrush flats and oak, chaparral and grassy savannah regions; throughout southwestern California from the coast to 7000 ft and on Santa Cruz Island.

Western Rattlesnake

Crotalus oreganus

Length: average 16–40 in; up to 4 ft and rarely to 5 ft

Generally unappreciated by humans, the rattlesnake plays an important ecological role, preying upon rodents and other small mammals. California's only native venomous snake has a bite that is painful but rarely lethal to an adult unless left untreated for several hours. • The rattlesnake is born live with a "button" rattle, to which an additional segment is added with each molt. • The red diamond rattlesnake *(C. rubber)* overlaps with the western rattlesnake in San Diego County. **Where found:** dry mountain areas and the interior valleys; from Santa Barbara County south to the Mexican border and east to desert slopes of the Transverse and Peninsular ranges as well as on Santa Cruz and Santa Catalina islands. **Also known as:** Pacific rattlesnake; formerly known as *C. viridis.*

Common Gartersnake

Thamnophis sirtalis

Length: 15–50 in

Swift on land and in water, the common gartersnake is an efficient hunter of amphibians, fish, small mammals, slugs and leeches. Some populations have shown resistance to the toxins produced by the western toad and the California newt and will prey upon them as well. • A single female can give birth to a litter of 3-83 young but typically has no more than 18. • There are many species of gartersnake in Southern California. **Where found:** aquatic and riparian habitats from sea level to just over 7000 ft; along the coast from Santa Barbara to San Diego counties.

126

Gophersnake

Pituophis catenifer

Length: 2½–6 ft

This large, beautiful constrictor is often mistaken for a rattlesnake because of its similar coloration, patterning and aggressive defensive strategy. When threatened, it hisses and vibrates its tail against vegetation, often producing a rattling sound. • The gophersnake frequently overwinters in communal dens with other snakes, including rattlesnakes, gartersnakes and racers. **Where found:** open, dry, oak savannahs, brushy chaparral, meadows and sparse, sunny areas in coniferous forests and deserts; throughout Southern California with various subspecies identified for separate regions. **Also known as:** bullsnake.

Kingsnake

Lampropeltis getula

Length: 24–45 in

The non-venomous kingsnake has several color and pattern phases, primarily of alternating bands or longitudinal stripes of black or brown against white or yellow, or sometimes combinations of both patterns with marbled, spotted or blotched coloring. The scales are smooth and glossy. • The kingsnake feeds on other reptiles, including rattlesnakes, to whose venom it is immune, as well as amphibians, bird nestlings and eggs and small mammals. **Where found:** near water and farming areas, oak savannahs, mixed pine-oak woodlands and brushy chaparral; throughout Southern California.

California Whipsnake

Masticophis lateralis

Length: 2½–5 ft

This high-strung, energetic snake moves about with its head held high, investigating its surroundings. Quick and agile, offering a challenging race to its pursuers, it preys mainly upon lizards but will not reject other types of prey such as insects, snakes, small mammals, frogs, birds and their nestlings. • The underbelly of this snake is yellow, turning a distinct pink under the length of the tail. **Where found:** brushy chaparral of rocky foothills, often along streams; southwestern California from the coast into the mountain ranges. **Also known as:** striped racer; *Coluber lateralis*.

FISH

Fish are ectothermic vertebrates that live in the water, have streamlined bodies covered in scales, and possess fins and gills. A fundamental feature of fish is the serially repeated set of vertebrae and segmented muscles that allow the animal to move from side to side, propelling it through the water. A varying number of fins (depending on the species) further aid the fish to swim and navigate. Most fish are oviparous and lay eggs that are fertilized externally. Eggs are either produced in vast quantities and then scattered, or they are laid in a spawning nest (redd) under rocks or logs. Parental care may be present in the defense of such a nest or territory. Spawning can involve migrating vast distances back to freshwater spawning grounds after spending 2–3 years in the ocean.

Salmon & Trout
p. 129

Pricklebacks
p. 130

Gobies
p. 130

Sculpin
p. 131

Grunion
p. 131

Stingrays
p. 131

Cutthroat Trout

Oncorhynchus clarki

Length: 8–12 in

Named for the red streak-
ing in the skin under the
lower jaw, cutthroat trout seen in the water can be
mistakenly identified as the similar-looking rainbow trout. The cutthroat's reddish
belly and throat become brighter during spawning. Females excavate redds with
their tails in late spring or early summer. • There are 3 native subspecies of cutthroat
trout in California. Some populations are coastal, others are freshwater residents and
some travel between the brackish estuaries and the freshwater tributaries. **Where
found:** saltwater and freshwater habitats from the Eel River drainage northward.

Rainbow Trout

Oncorhynchus mykiss

Length: 7½–18 in

The different popula-
tions of rainbow trout
in California have dif-
ferent life history
behaviors. Coastal rain-
bow trout, also called steelhead
trout, spend a portion of their life cycle in the ocean, returning to freshwater
streams to spawn. Summer steelhead trout enter their natal rivers in spring or
summer and hold there until winter or spring, when they spawn; other steelhead
trout enter the river in fall or winter and spawn in late winter or early spring.
Coastal streams may support both steelhead and freshwater residents. **Where
found:** saltwater and freshwater habitats; along the entire coast and inland to the
Sacramento–San Joaquin system. **Also known as:** steelhead trout.

Brook Trout

Salvelinus fontinalis

Length: 10 in

Colorful and feisty, the brook trout is a prized sport fish
introduced from eastern North America. It is known to interbreed with other species
of trout, and strong management practices must be put into place to protect native
fish. The brown trout *(Salmo trutta)* is another popular sport fish, introduced to the
United States in 1893 from Europe. • The brook trout is a type of char. It is a fall
spawner and is capable of reproducing in the substrate of high mountain lakes,
whereas other trout species require clean gravel beds in flowing water. **Where found:**
freshwater habitats; widespread throughout Southern California's mountain lakes.

Black Prickleback

Xiphister atropurpureus

Length: up to 12 in

Although it looks and acts similar to an eel, the black prickleback is not a true eel. It often slithers out of the water under rocks and seaweed, able to breathe air as long as it is relatively moist. It can stay out of water for about 10 hours, possibly more. • The black prickleback spawns off the central California coast from February to April. The male guards the nest of 738–4070 eggs. **Where found:** saltwater habitats; close to rocky shores with algal cover; under rocks and in gravel areas; lower intertidal and shallow subtidal zones down to depths of 26 ft; small individuals are common in tide pools all along the coast. **Also known as:** black blenny.

Blackeye Goby

Rhinogobiops nicholsii

Length: up to 6 in

Frequently seen by sport divers, gobies have interesting colors and patterns and large eyes. The blackeye goby is less colorful than many other gobies, but it has distinctive black, bulbous eyes that contrast with its pale body. A black border to the dorsal fin (and the pectoral fin of breeding males) is a diagnostic feature. • It nests from April to September, laying 500–3000 eggs over the spawning season, and is very territorial against other blackeye gobies. **Where found:** saltwater habitats; sand- and mud-bottomed waters near rocky areas and reefs, in bays and in deep waters all along the coast. **Also known as:** *Coryphopterus nicholsi.*

Longjaw Mudsucker

Gillichthys mirabilis

Length: up to 8 in

If you enjoy squishing your toes in the mud after the tide goes out, you may get your toe tickled by a mudsucker. This little fish is commonly found stranded in shallow pools or burrowed into the cool wet slime of muddy banks along quiet bays and estuaries. It has a distinctively large mouth with a lower jaw that extends back to its gills; the male is proud of this feature, flaunting it by opening and inflating it as much as possible—analogous to muscle flexing to intimidate other males. Two mudsuckers showing off in this manner might look like they are kissing, but they are actually battling over territory. **Where found:** tidal flats, bays, estuaries and sloughs all along the coast.

Wooly Sculpin

Clinocottus analis

Length: up to 7 in

At each low tide you can find
an array of tiny fish swimming about
the tide pools, but the one you are most likely to see is the
wooly sculpin. Maturing individuals have been proven to return to favored tide
pools, remembering and navigating their way amongst the waves. They feed on
the smaller creatures caught in the tide pools with them and will eat just about
anything that they can fit into their mouths. Another common tide pool resident
is the rockpool blenny *(Hypsoblennius gilberti)*, distinguishable by its single long
dorsal fin rather than the 2 fins of the sculpin. **Where found:** tide pools and rocky,
gravely shores all along the coast.

Grunion

Leuresthes tenuis

Length: up to 7½ in

The running of the grunions
is an amazing event to
observe; crowds of people line
the beaches to watch the thousands of little fish that come ashore when the
moon is full and the tide is high to lay their eggs in the sand. Their silvery bodies
glint in the moonlight as they wriggle about after being washed ashore by a large wave
and then quickly dig their way into the sand before the next wave comes along. The
females dig in deep so that only their heads are left sticking up out of the sand; they lay
their eggs, and on the next wave a male, or two, will wrap around the female to insem-
inate the eggs. Both parents then ride the next wave back out to sea. The eggs hatch 10
days later on the next high tide, which carries the fry into the ocean. **Where found:**
sandy beaches along open shorelines with uninhibited wave action all along the coast.

Round Stingray

Urolphus halleri

Length: up to 22 in

During the summer months, these little stingrays are
found close to shore skimming along the sand. Stingrays
are docile and do not attack people, but swimmers have been
stung by accidentally stepping on them. To avoid this painful
experience, shuffle your feet as you move along the sand so the
stingray has a chance to swim out of your way. Several aquariums in Southern
California have "petting" tanks of stingrays, which actually seem to enjoy being
stroked. • Stingrays eat crabs, shrimps, snails and crustaceans. **Where found:**
shallows of quiet bays and estuaries all along the coast; buried into the surface of
the sand when at rest.

INVERTEBRATES

M ore than 95 percent of animal species on the planet are invertebrates, and there are thousands of invertebrate species in California. The few mentioned in this guide are frequently encountered and easily recognizable. Invertebrates can be found in a variety of habitats and are an important part of most ecosystems. They provide food for a variety of land and marine animals. Terrestrial invertebrates also play an important role in the pollination of plants and aid in the decay process.

Seashells
pp. 134–35

Sea Slug
p. 136

Sea Cucumber
p. 136

Sea Stars
pp. 136–37

Sand Dollars & Sea Urchins
p. 137

Anemones, Coral & Sponges
pp. 138–39

Jellyfish
p. 139

Squid
p. 139

Crustaceans
pp. 140–41

Butterflies & Moths
pp. 142–44

Dragonflies
pp. 145–46

Wasps & Bees
p. 146

Beetles
p. 147

Ants
p. 147

Crane Flies
p. 147

Cicadas & Grigs
p. 148

Mantids & Cockroaches
pp. 148–49

Non-Insect Arthropods
pp. 149–50

Giant Owl Limpet

Lottia gigantea

Length: up to 4½ in

"Giant" is a relative term, but this little limpet does push its weight around, bullying away smaller limpets. It stakes out its territory of about 1 ft² and will literally push other species of limpets out. Once it has cleared its space of pesky neighbors, it has a fine garden of algae to sustain itself on. When not grazing, the giant owl limpet positions itself within a groove that it carves into a rock, which it then tightly clamps itself against. **Where found:** on exposed rocks in heavy surf areas between high- and low-tide lines all along the coast.

Black Abalone

Haliotis cracherodii

Length: 6 in

There are several species of abalone in our local coastal waters; most are highly prized commercially and have been overharvested. To prevent over-exploitation, several restrictions have been put in place to protect them. Red abalones (*H. rufescens*) are the largest and most prized. Black abalones are edible but are not fished commercially and thus, luckily, remain fairly abundant. • Black abalones feed mainly on large brown algae. • Never cut an abalone off its rock; they are hemophiliacs and will bleed to death if cut. **Where found:** deep crevices in rocks between high- and low-tide lines to water 20 ft deep all along the coast.

Black Tegula

Tegula funebralis

Length: 1 in

These snails are some of the most abundant on the Pacific Coast. Large individuals are known to live 20–30 years. They take advantage of sloped substrates to flee predators such as sea stars by pulling inside their shells and rolling away. • Empty black tegula shells are a favorite home acquisition of hermit crabs. **Where found:** on rocky shores between high- and low-tide lines all along the coast. **Also known as:** turban tegula.

California Mussel

Mytilus californianus

Length: 10 in

California mussels are the most conspicuous and abundant animals on our shores. They are predominant in the upper tidal zone and occur in massive growths. Mussels are capable of limited locomotion but rarely move from their practically permanent position; they attach to a substrate by byssal threads produced by their foot. • Sea stars, crabs, shorebirds and sea otters are among the mussel's top predators, but the supreme enthusiasts of this tasty mollusk are humans. **Where found:** on rocks, wharf pilings and unprotected shores, from well above the low-tide line to water 80 ft deep all along the coast.

Lined Chiton

Tonicella lineate

Length: 2 in

The gorgeous lined chiton sports an array of fashionable shells typically mottled reddish brown as a background and decorated with zigzag lines patterned across it in colors varying from light and dark reds to blues, browns, black or white. The fleshy girdle that surrounds the 8-sectioned plate of armor (chitons are the only mollusk with jointed shells) is usually greenish or yellowish. **Where found:** on rocks covered with coralline algae; underneath purple sea urchins; from the low-tide line to depths of 180 ft all along the coast.

Bean Clam

Donax gouldi

Length: up to 1 in

With their variety of shell colors (which often includes banding designs), bean clams are fun to collect and are often scattered on wave-washed sandy beaches. In some years they have population explosions and the beaches can be littered with shells. When alive, these little clams live buried just below the surface of the sand and prefer beaches that are well ravaged by wave action. Similar species—such as the wedge clam (*D. californicus*), which prefers beaches with calmer wave action—are found in various beach environs. **Where found:** sandy, wave-washed beaches all along the coast.

Opalescent Nudibranch

Hermissenda crassicornis

Length: up to 3 in

This colorful sea slug is relatively common along the entire Pacific Coast. It is distinguishable by the vivid orange line down the middle of its back; the rest of its body is variable with beautiful colors and markings. • Sea slugs are predatory, hunting small anemones, bryozoans, sea squirts, worms and other small creatures. They store the stinging cells of sea anemones at the ends of their own cerata (the hair-like projections on the body) to use for their own defense purposes—often against another nudibranch in a territorial dispute. **Where found:** rocky shores, tide pools and eelgrass beds all along the coast.

Dwarf Sea Cucumber

Lissothuria nutriens

Length: to 1 in

Named after a salad item, sea cucumbers are not plants but animals, related to sea stars and sea urchins. They are most often colorful and covered in rough bumps, with a ring of tentacles protruding from the mouth to catch particles of food in the water. Sea cucumbers are detritivores, feeding on dead and decaying organic material—in California they feed mainly on kelp shed. • As a defense mechanism, and no doubt effectively repulsive, sea cucumbers can spit out their guts and regenerate them. **Where found:** algal holdfasts, surf grass roots and encrusted rocks.

Bat Star

Patiria miniata

Radius: 6–8 in

The bat star is the most abundant sea star on the West Coast. This species is highly variable in color—from reddish orange or purple to green, often with mottled patterns—and form, with 5 (sometimes 4–9) short, thick arms. • Sea stars feed on bivalves, wrapping around them and forcing them out of their shells, and will scavenge dead fish. Their predators include other sea stars, mollusks and crustaceans, all of which are often deterred by the bat star's distasteful chemical secretions. **Where found:** kelp forests; on rocks or sand from the low-tide line to depths of 960 ft.

Ochre Sea Star

Pisaster ochraceus

Radius: 10 in

Beautiful yellow, orange, brown, reddish or purple ochre sea stars often suffer from over-collection by beachcombers who unfortunately do not realize that this color is lost once the sea star dies and dries up. • Ochre sea stars are a keystone predatory species whose absence in an ecosystem causes visible shifts in the numbers, types and dominances of other species. These sea stars are abundant on beds of mussels, their favored prey, and are preyed upon by gulls and sea otters. **Where found:** intertidal areas; wave-washed, rocky shores at the low-tide line.

Eccentric Sand Dollar

Dendraster excentricus

Radius: 1½ in

Beachcombers are most familiar with this sand dollar as a smooth, spineless, gray specimen with a 5-petaled flower design in the center of its surface. In its living form, it is furry in appearance, and its color varies from light lavender-gray to brown or reddish brown to dark purple-black. • The eccentric sand dollar colonizes sandy ocean floors, stabilizing the strata. In rough waters, it buries itself under the sand for protection. • Sand dollars are closely related to sea urchins. **Where found:** sandy bottoms of sheltered bays and open coasts, from the low-tide line to depths of 130 ft.

Purple Sea Urchin

Strongylocentrotus purpuratus

Radius: 2 in without spines

In large populations, the purple sea urchin and the red sea urchin (*S. franciscanus*) are capable of overgrazing and destroying the important kelp forests off the coast of California, a situation that a healthy population of sea otters, the urchin's main predator, keeps in check. • The sea urchin is a delicacy of Japanese cuisine and is becoming increasingly popular in California's sushi restaurants. It is also eaten fresh from the shell, much like an oyster, at fishing ports and wharves. • Adult purple sea urchins are a vivid purple, but the juveniles are green. **Where found:** from the low-tide line and rocky shores into kelp forests in waters up to 300 ft deep.

Aggregating Anemone

Anthopleura elegantissima

Height: *Aggregating individuals:* 6 in;
Solitary individuals: 20 in
Width: *Aggregating individuals:* 3 in;
Solitary individuals: 10 in

This sea anemone has 5 rings of tentacles with tips varying in delicate colors of pink, lavender and blue. The aggregating form is in fact a colony of clones created by the "founding" anemone, which divides itself in a form of asexual reproduction. These clones tolerate proximity to each other because they are not competing genetically. If a genetically different individual were in proximity, they would lash out with their tentacles, wounding or killing it. Their toxins are completely benign to their clones. **Where found:** rock walls, boulders or pilings from intertidal to low-tide zones.

Giant Green Anemone

Anthopleura xanthogrammica

Height: 12 in
Width: 10 in

The giant green anemone is a solitary giant but is not antisocial. Often within tentacle-tip distance of another anemone, it makes contact every once in a while as if to reassure itself that is it not alone. • Its column varies from green to brown, and the thick, short, tapered tentacles vary from green or blue to white, in rows of 6 or more. The green coloring is enhanced by a symbiotic relationship with green algae, from which the anemone obtains photosynthetic by-products. **Where found:** exposed coastlines; on rocks, seawalls and pilings in tide pools and to depths of more than 50 ft.

Orange Cup Coral

Balanophyllia elegans

Height: ½ in
Width: ½ in

Orange cup coral is the only stony coral in the intertidal zone of the Pacific Coast from British Columbia to Baja California. It has a stony, cup-shaped skeleton in which the base of the animal is set, and 36 long, tapered, translucent tentacles reach out and contract back within the skeleton. The tentacles have masses of stinging cells dotted along them, so do not touch this bright orange beauty. The fluorescent pigment is bright even at depths of 30 ft or more. **Where found:** in shaded waters, such as under ledges and boulders, from the low-tide line down to depths of 70 ft all along the coast.

Purple Sponge

Haliclona permollis

Height: 1½ in
Width: 36 in

Looking like a bubblegum-colored lava flow, this
encrusting sponge spills over rocks and within
tide pools. Its smooth, soft form seems to bubble
with little raised volcanoes that reach up to ¼ in higher
than the surface of the sponge. • Sponges reproduce either by budding (a tip is
released or breaks off and regenerates upon attachment to a new site) or by releasing
tiny clusters of cells that germinate on a new site. Sponges are also capable of sexual
reproduction, releasing sperm into the water that then fertilizes eggs in another
sponge; the larvae swim to a new site, attach and develop into a tiny sponge.
Where found: sheltered waters from the intertidal zone to depths of 20 ft.

Sea Gooseberry

Pleurobrachia bachei

Bell diameter: up to 1 in
Tentacle length: up to 6 in

A member of a group of jellyfish called "comb jellies,"
the delicate sea gooseberry is an open-ocean dwell-
ing creature but is at the mercy of the currents
and can be tossed ashore after a storm. After such
events, you may find beaches littered with these
little blobs of jelly; if you find one still alive, you can put it in a glass of sea water and
observe its delicate features: 8 lines (or combs) of cilia that reflect and defract light
as they beat, long graceful tentacles armed with sticky cells to catch prey, and faintly
perceptible internal organs visible through the transparent body. **Where found:**
open inshore and offshore waters, or stranded on the beach.

Opalescent Squid

Loligo opalescens

Length: up to 12 in

During the breeding season, these
squid come inshore and attach egg sacs to the ocean
floor (which can sometimes be observed washed ashore and look
like 6-inch-long sacs of jelly). Squid are able to quickly change color to disguise
themselves against the substrate and hide from predators; a school of squid will
change color together, and this species in particular is noted for an opalescent
pale green coloration that gives it a shimmering effect. If extremely distressed, the
squid will release a cloud of ink to hide behind and then escape from the threat.
People as well as sea-lions and several sea birds eat squid. **Where found:** open
ocean, near kelp beds.

Giant Acorn Barnacle

Balnus nubilis

Radius: up to 2 in

We typically see this barnacle when it is closed; however, when it feeds—which is rarely and sometimes not for months at a time—long, feathery plumes reach out from the top of the barnacle shell to filter bits of organic matter from the water. • This barnacle must remain almost continuously covered by water or it can easily desiccate. • Capable of sexual reproduction yet immobile, this animal has the largest penis-to-body-size ratio in the animal kingdom so that the male can reach his mate. **Where found:** rocky shores and exposed coasts; lower intertidal areas with continuous water cover; subtidal to depths of 300 ft.

Red Rock Shrimp

Lysmata californica

Length: up to 2¾ in

Of the many shrimp that can be found in the tide pools of Southern California, the red rock shrimp is one of the most common. Many shrimp species look very similar to each other, but the red rock shrimp is distinctly light beige or cream-colored with red stripes that make it look mostly red. • Shrimp are best observed at night with a flashlight, but this species can also be seen picking at parasites and dead skin on fish and eels, and will even attempt this service on the fingers of divers. **Where found:** from the low-tide line to depths of 50 ft.

California Beach Flea

Megalorchestia californiana

Length: 1 in

Flea is a misnomer for this creature because the beach flea is actually a small crustacean, but its habit of hopping about the beach in significant numbers brings to mind an infestation. These little creatures are harmless; they do not bite and are rarely on the beach during the hot daytime hours, preferring to burrow into the sand or piles of drying kelp to avoid the sun. By night, however, they are known for their all-night beach parties when they come out by the thousands to feast on kelp that has been freshly washed ashore. **Where found:** sandy beaches from Laguna Beach northward.

Striped Shore Crab
Pachygrapsus crassipes

Width: up to 2½ in

The striped shore crab can be found scuttling sideways just about any-where along the coast, from rocky shorelines to tidal estuaries, scavenging animal matter and grazing on the film of algae growing on the rocks. It hides under the rocks and burrows into the mud for shelter and is quite tolerant of remaining dry for extended periods without desiccating. • There are several species of shore crabs in our area; they have a similar body shape but different coloration, such as purple and yellow of the purple shore crab (*Hemigrapsus nudus*) and the yellow shore crab (*H. oregonensis*). **Where found:** open rocky shores, among seaweeds and in shallow, protected waters.

Blue-handed Hermit Crab

Pagurus samuelis

Length: ¾ in

Hermit crabs do not produce their own shells, and only the front portion of their bodies is armored; they must protect the soft regions of their bodies by acquiring discarded snail shells. The black tegula shell is one of the preferred shells for this little crab to use as a home. If the crab outgrows its current shell or finds a more suitable and otherwise unoccupied one, it will relocate. **Where found:** permanent tide pools of the intertidal zone.

California Spiny Lobster

Panuliris interruptus

Length: up to 30 in

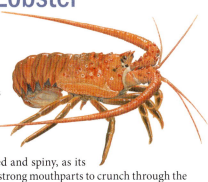

This species is highly sought after by commercial lobster fishermen off the coast of California, and recreational divers can even go out on lobster dives to try to catch them. This prized delicacy is a popular menu item in local restau-rants, making large individuals in the wild hard to come by. • This lobster is red and spiny, as its name suggests, and instead of claws it has strong mouthparts to crunch through the tough body parts of its animal prey. **Where found:** rocky shores, under seaweed and rocks. **Also known as:** langosta.

Western Tiger Swallowtail

Papilio rutulus

Wingspan: 3¼–3½ in

The "tail" of the swallowtail is defensive. If a bird attacks, it will grab at this extension, sparing the butterfly's body. This butterfly is often seen with the lower half of its wings missing, implying that the strategy must indeed work. • There are several species of swallowtail in California with various colorations, but the western tiger never seems to go unnoticed or without a compliment from its observer. The caterpillar is also stunning, sporting a smooth, green body with bright yellow and blue eyespots at one end. It feeds on poplar trees. **Where found:** along watercourses and in gardens.

Monarch

Danaus plexippus

Wingspan: 3¾ in

The regal monarch is California's most famous butterfly, known for its wide distribution and incredible migration. Millions of monarchs overwinter as adults in the mountain forests of Southern California and Mexico. With warmer temperatures, adults migrate northward, laying eggs in patches of milkweed plants. These eggs quickly develop into adults, which continue north as far as the Canadian Rockies. • Toxic compounds in the milkweed make this insect unpalatable to birds, and the birds remember the coloration of the monarch to avoid it in the future. Many butterflies mimic the monarch's coloration to deter the same predators. **Where found:** milkweed patches and flower meadows.

Gulf Fritillary

Boloria epithore

Wingspan: up to 1½ in

Fritillary is a name that refers to a large group of orange-and-black butterflies in North America and Europe. They are distinguishable from each other by the pattern and number of spots and designs on their wings. When they alight upon a flower to feed on the nectar, they spread their wings wide open in the sun, making them popular subjects to photograph. **Where found:** meadows and clearings.

West Coast Lady

Vanessa annabella

Wingspan: about 2 in

There are 3 species of "lady" in California; this species is more commonly seen in the lowlands and is found year-round near the coast. It goes through several generations in a single year and is easy to rear, making it popular in schoolrooms. Massive migrations can be observed elsewhere on the continent when populations of this insect come to the West Coast to escape cold winter weather in other parts of North America. **Where found:** lowland gardens, vacant lots.

California Sister

Adelpha bredowii

Wingspan: about 3⅓ in

This species, commonly called simply "sister" (in the east it was once called Arizona sister), is widespread throughout North America. California probably has more animal species named after it than any other state, even if the animal ranges beyond California's borders. • The caterpillars feed on leaves of most trees but are fond of oaks, and the adults also eat aphid honeydew off tree leaves. They often rest with their wings spread fully open, giving you a chance to see their lovely patterns and colors. **Where found:** wooded areas, gardens and parks.

Mourning Cloak

Nymphalis antiopa

Wingspan: approx. 3 in

Mourning cloaks are one of the longest living butterflies, living for up to a full year (most butterflies live mere days or weeks, rarely months), and are tolerant of cool temperatures. Adults emerge from their pupae in mid- to late summer and may overwinter under bark, debris or even a window shutter, but if temperatures are above freezing they can be seen even in winter. They emerge from hibernation in spring to mate and lay eggs. The caterpillars feed with enthusiasm on aspen and willow trees. **Where found:** openings in forested areas.

143

Snowberry Clearwing

Hemaris diffinis

Wingspan: 1½ in

This bizarre little insect often fools people into thinking that it is a small hummingbird by the way it hovers around flowers. Its long proboscis, furred body and handsome coloring warrant a closer inspection to affirm that is indeed a moth, actually a member of the sphinx moth family. • Active in the daytime, unusual for a moth, it feeds among the flowers much like a butterfly; its caterpillar feeds on a variety of forest plants. **Where found:** widespread. **Also known as:** hummingbird moth, bumblebee moth.

White-lined Sphinx

Lyles lineata

Wingspan: 3½ in

This nocturnal moth feeds on flower nectar and will sometimes remain quiet and still amongst the foliage of plants during the day. It has a very long proboscis to probe into deep flowers, such as honeysuckle. The caterpillar is typically black and green, very large in size and often poses with its head upright in the manner of the sphinx, hence the analogous name. The caterpillar burrows into the soil to form a pupa. **Where found:** widespread from urban gardens to deserts.

Black Witch

Ascalapha odorata

Wingspan: up to 6 in

Migrating into our area in summer from Central America, this large moth migrates all along the Pacific Northwest, making a longer migration than the famous monarch. It feeds on sap and over-ripe fruit. If you want to get a chance to see some of the beautiful moths in our area, and attract them with something other than a lightbulb around which they fly erratically and are difficult to observe, you can set up a bait of their favored foods—some bug enthusiasts make a mixture of beer, molasses, rum and brown sugar, heated up to melt the sugars and then painted onto the bark of a tree. **Where found:** forested areas, on tropical acacias.

Boreal Bluet

Enallagma boreale

Length: 1¼ in

Nearly every pond or lake will host this familiar
blue damselfly. The female may sometimes be
green or yellow, but the male is always blue.
Several other species of bluet are also found
in our area and are quite difficult to tell
apart. To distinguish a damselfly from
a dragonfly, however, notice that damsel-
flies are thin, and all 4 of their wings are similar in
shape and are (usually) folded up over their backs.
Where found: among reeds in ponds and lakes.

Green Darner

Anex junius

Length: up to 3 in

The green darner is a wonderful sight,
especially in spring when this migratory
insect arrives with the message of warmer days to
come. In late summer, it breeds and lays its eggs in
ponds and shallow lakes, and by fall the next generation has hatched and is soon ready to make a return
migration south. The warm climate of parts of
Southern California accommodates green darners
year-round, but different populations move in and
out of the area. **Where found**: near ponds and lakes.

Variegated Meadowhawk

Sympetrum corruptum

Length: 1½ in

As with so many things in nature, we still have a lot
to learn when it comes to variegated meadowhawks.
These widespread dragonflies stage a mass migration
on the West Coast in fall. They are
observed heading south, but it
is yet unknown where they travel
to, where they came from prior to congregating
en masse, or even what triggers them to know
when to do so. Some experts are studying whether fall
wind patterns give the dragonflies environmental clues as to their
travel date. **Where found:** ponds and lakes; prefers stagnant waters.

145

Yellow Jackets

Vespula spp.

Length: ½–¾ in

Amazing engineers of paper architecture, yellow jackets chew on bark or wood and mix it with saliva to make the pulp. Large sheets of paper line the nest in which 6-sided paper chambers hold the larvae. Different types of wood create swirls of color—grays and browns—inadvertently adding some artistic style to the structure. The nest can reach the size of a basketball by the end of summer; only the queen, however, will survive winter—the only safe time of year to get a close-up look at a wasp nest without being stung by one of the architects. **Where found:** nests in high branches or in abandoned animal burrows; widespread throughout California. **Also known as:** paper wasp, hornet.

Bumble Bees

Bombus spp.

Length: ¼–¾ in

Bees have long inspired our admiration and appreciation; throughout history, the image of the bee appears on ancient coins; in Masonic, Mormon, Pagan, Egyptian, Jewish and Greek symbology; as an icon of royalty in Sudan, Niger, France and India; as a personal emblem adopted by Napoleon Bonaparte; as a sacred feminine symbol of the Cult of Athena; and as an embodiment of the goddess Venus—just to name a few examples! Bumble bees do sting but have a docile temperament and are slow to anger; if they are forced to sting, the act typically causes their death. The queen will establish a colony in an abandoned mouse or vole burrow, in which the worker bees create wax combs to rear grubs and produce honey. **Where found:** clearings and meadows wherever there are flowering plants; region wide.

Carpenter Bees

Xylocopa spp.

Length: up to 1 in

Carpenter bees pollinate flowers by seeking out the pollen and nectar but get their name from their ability to chew through wood. They don't eat wood, however; their wood chewing is the way they make their nests. They burrow into dead wood, such as fallen trees, fence posts or even wooden buildings. The nest is a series of larval cells that form a dead-end tunnel. Bees of many species are sometimes seen chewing through the bottom of a flower to obtain the nectar; this shortcut does not allow the flower to become pollinated. **Where found:** widespread in a variety of habitats.

Convergent Ladybug

Hippodamia convergens

Length: ¼ in

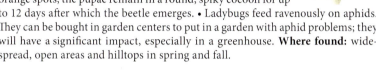

There are several species of ladybug, all distinguishable from each other by their size, number of spots and coloration, which do not change in size or number as the insect ages. Some ladybugs are not even red. • The convergent ladybug is the most common, and it is easily recognized by its black and white head and red or orange wings (called elytra) with 13 black spots. The larvae are black with orange spots; the pupae remain in a round, spiky cocoon for up to 12 days after which the beetle emerges. • Ladybugs feed ravenously on aphids. They can be bought in garden centers to put in a garden with aphid problems; they will have a significant impact, especially in a greenhouse. **Where found:** widespread, open areas and hilltops in spring and fall.

Carpenter Ants

Camponotus spp.

Length: ½ in

Similar but unrelated to termites, carpenter ants bore through wood to construct their homes in trees, and sometimes in our wooden homes as well. Watch for a pile of sawdust in either case. • These ants are the largest in our area, and they are preyed upon by our largest woodpeckers, pileated woodpeckers. • Carpenter ants do not sting as do other ant species, but their powerful, woodchewing jaws are capable of a strong bite. **Where found:** forested areas.

Crane Flies

Holorusia spp.

Length: up to 1½ in

These innocent insects are not giant mosquitoes or garden harvestmen ("daddy longlegs") but very benign and harmless crane flies. Crane flies do not bite, and their larvae only scavenge in soil and rotting logs. • The crane is an appropriate analogy for these long-legged creatures, which are more comfortable in the forest than when they accidentally find themselves inside your house. **Where found:** forested areas.

Cicada

Family Cicadidae

Length: ¾ in

Take a walk in sagebrush country in mid-summer, and the fields will be resonating with the music of the male cicada. The loud, prolonged, dry, rattling buzz is made by a vibration in the insect's abdomen. • The larvae live underground for years, feeding on roots until they finally emerge one summer, ready to make some noise. • The species in the West do not often reproduce to the infesting numbers that can famously occur in the East, nor are these insects locusts, which are a type of grasshopper. **Where found:** dry, forested or shrubby areas, particularly in sagebrush country in the northeast of the state.

Jerusalem Cricket

Stenopelmatus fuscus

Length: up to 2 in

This nocturnal grig is a perpetual scavenger that will steal a meal wherever it can find one—it eats garbage, vegetables from gardens, roots and tubers, carrion or any prey opportunity it encounters. It requires moist soil to burrow in by day and is most active in spring. • This cricket's large head and fat abdomen are distinctive and give it a human-like appearance that made it a character in native folk tales and superstitions. **Where found:** widespread in moist habitats. **Also known as:** potato bug, sand cricket, Chacos, children of the Earth.

California Mantid

Stagomomantis californica

Length: 2½ in

No matter what its color—green, yellow or brown—a mantid is always admired. Its slow, deliberate movements are analogous to tai chi martial arts movements, and this insect's ability to move its "neck" to observe a passing object or our own human gaze is somewhat human-like. The praying mantid (*Mantid religionsa*) is also in our area. **Where found:** dry, shrubby areas.

German Cockroach

Blatella germanica

Length: ½ in

An unwelcome visitor to our kitchens and bath-
rooms, this cockroach seeks out damp areas and
obtains its minimal water requirements merely
from condensation. It is a notorious scavenger, eating just about anything it can find. Despite its dirty
reputation, the German cockroach is not a carrier of
disease; it is typically found in abundance in those
areas where we have created our own filth. • This introduced species, like most,
has become a pest by finding a niche in urban environs; there are many native
species of cockroach in woodland habitats that are content to remain within their
own niche and avoid that of humans. **Where found:** buildings and dumpsters;
in association with human habitation throughout Southern California.

Scorpion

Order Scorpionida

Length: 1½ in

This well-recognized creature of deserts
and Mediterranean climates is feared for the
deadly venomous sting that is given by a species
called the black scorpion (*Centruroides sculpturatura-
tus*) native to Arizona; most other scorpions, including those more typically found
in California, are not dangerous and deliver a sting no worse than that of a hornet.
• Scorpions tend to be nocturnal, when they actively hunt small insects; by day they
stay sheltered under rocks. • Under UV light, scorpions glow green. **Where found:**
dry, open areas.

Golden Orb Weaver

Argiope aurantia

Length: at least ½ in

The classic "orb" web of this spider is the most
familiar to us—flat with spirals of silk connected to
radiating spokes—and we admire it for its symmetry
and engineering. • This spider is completely harmless to people, though it has a voracious appetite for
insects that get caught in its web, which the spider
kills with a venomous bite. • The female is large and
lanky with lovely patterning, whereas the male is
about ¼ the size of the female and is inconspicuous,
living on an imperfect web beside that of his mate. **Where found:** gardens and
shrubby places. **Also known as:** yellow garden spider, common garden spider.

California Ebony Tarantula

Aphonopelma eutylenum

Length: up to 1¾ in

This secretive spider lives in crevices and burrows in grassy, open areas, but the male will venture out during the fall breeding season in search of a mate. • The California ebony tarantula is slow moving and prefers to wait for an insect to walk unwarily past the entrance of its burrow, where the spider can grab it. • This tarantula's venom is not dangerous to humans, and it is unlikely to bite in defense; rather, it will use its legs to flick the hairs from its abdomen at an attacker. The hairs are barbed and are very irritating to the skin. **Where found:** open areas; chaparral and grasslands.

Western Black Widow

Latrodectus hesperus

Length: *Male:* up to ¼ in;
Female: up to ½ in

Not known for its web-making skills, the black widow makes a disorganized mass of web in the abandoned burrows of small mammals. If seen out of hiding, the western black widow is easy to identify by its shiny, large, black body with a red hourglass-shaped marking on the underside of the abdomen. • The bite of a black widow is dangerous and best avoided. • The female really does often eat the male after mating, but the black widow is not the only spider to do so. **Where found:** dry, well-drained areas.

PLANTS

Plants belong to the Kingdom Plantae. They are autotrophic, which means that they produce their own food from inorganic materials through a process called photosynthesis. Plants are the basis of all food webs. They supply oxygen to the atmosphere, modify climate, and create and hold down soil. They disperse their seeds and pollen through carriers such as wind or animals. Fossil fuels come from ancient deposits of organic matter—largely that of plants. In this book, plants are separated into 3 categories: trees, shrubs and herbs and other plants.

TREES

Trees are long-lived, woody plants that are normally taller than 16 ft. There are 2 types of trees: coniferous and broadleaf. Conifers, or cone-bearers, have needles or small, scale-like leaves. Most conifers are evergreens, but some species, such as larches, shed their leaves in winter. Most broadleaf trees lose their leaves in fall and are known as deciduous trees (meaning "falling off" in Latin). Some exceptions include rhododendrons and several hollies.

Trees are important to a variety of ecosystems. A single tree can provide a home or a food source for many different animals. A group of trees can provide a windbreak, camouflage or shelter, hold down soil and control runoff. A forest that is large and diverse in its structure and composition defines the community of species that live within it. Old-growth forest is critical habitat for many species that use the fallen or hollowed out trees as nesting or denning sites. Fallen, decomposing logs also provide habitat for mosses, fungi and invertebrates. The logs eventually completely degrade into nutrient-rich soil. Large forests retain carbon dioxide, an important preventive factor of global warming, and responsibly managed forests can sustain an industry that provides wood products and jobs.

Firs & Pines
pp. 153–55

Cedar & Cypress
p. 156

Sequoia
p. 157

Oaks
pp. 157–58

Cotton-wood
p. 159

Madrone
p. 159

Maple
p. 160

California Laurel
p. 160

Blue Palo Verde
p. 161

California Fan Palm
p. 162

Joshua Tree
p. 162

Eucalyptus
p. 163

California Buckeye
p. 163

White Fir

Abies concolor

Height: 130–180 ft
Needles: 2–3 in long
Seed cones: 3–5½ in long

White fir is a popular Christmas tree and has a fragrance that creates nostalgia for the holiday season. Foresters don't often view this tree with the same fondness because it is shade tolerant and out-competes sugar pines and incense cedars. In addition, its low-hanging limbs are a fire hazard, inviting small fires to reach up to the canopy and threaten otherwise unreachable trees such as the giant sequoia. • This tree's soft, knotty wood is used commercially only for pulp and cheap construction materials. **Where found:** mountain slopes. **Also known as:** amabilis fir, Pacific silver fir.

Shore Pine

Pinus contorta

Height: up to 65 ft
Needles: 1–2¾ in long, in pairs
Seed cones: 1–2 in long

Shore pine does indeed grow near the shore and does not merely tolerate but seems to thrive in the salty sea spray and ocean winds, making it fairly common along the immediate coast where most other trees can't survive. This tough climate, however, causes this tenacious tree to grow twisted and stunted. • Native groups used the roots for rope, the bark for splints and the pitch for waterproofing or as a glue. **Where found:** closed pine forests, coastal strand, wetland-riparian areas, exposed outer-coastal shorelines, dunes, bogs and rocky hilltops. **Also known as:** beach pine.

Jeffrey Pine

Pinus jeffreyi

Height: up to 180 ft, more typically 100 ft
Needles: 5–11 in long, in 3s
Seed cones: 5½–11½ in long

Jeffrey pine superficially resembles ponderosa pine. The 2 species can be distinguished by smelling the resin: whereas ponderosa pine resin smells more like turpentine, Jeffrey pine resin has a scent similar to lemon or vanilla. The sweet scent comes from n-heptane, an unusual and volatile compound. Resin distillers back in the 1800s suffered random explosions until they discovered the compound and quickly learned to identify and avoid Jeffrey pines. • Western gray squirrels relish the ripe pine seeds, whereas deer, rabbits, pocket gophers and porcupines eat and destroy the young saplings. **Where found:** dry, cold mountain elevations where other pines suffer.

Sugar Pine

Pinus lambertiana

Height: 175–200 ft
Needles: 2–4½ in long, in bundles of 5
Seed cones: 9¾–19¾ in long

Sugar pine is the largest species of pine and has the longest cones of any conifer. Mature individuals occasionally surpass 500 years of age, with volumes second only to the giant sequoia. Famed naturalist John Muir considered the sugar pine the "king of conifers." • This pine gets its name from its sweet sap, which rivals that of maples, though this virtue has been unable to save it from the chainsaw. Sugar pine is heavily harvested beyond its regrowth potential. **Where found:** wide range of soil conditions typically associated with conifer-hardwood forests.

Yellow Pine

Pinus ponderosa

Height: 33–130 ft
Needles: 4–10 in long, in bundles of 3
Seed cones: 3–5½ in long

These stately pines thrive in areas that are periodically burned. • The straight, cinnamon colored trunks are distinctive, with black fissures outlining a jigsaw puzzle of thick plates of bark. • Native peoples ground the oil-rich seeds into meal and collected the sweet inner bark in spring, when the sap was running. Large scars can still be seen on some older trees, attesting to people's fondness for this sweet treat. • The cones have thick, dull brown scales tipped with a stiff prickle. **Where found:** mountains and foothills. **Also known as:** ponderosa pine.

Pinyon Pine

Pinus edulis

Height: 10–25 ft
Needles: 1–2 in
Seed cones: 2 in with edible pine nuts

The edible pine nuts from the cones of this pine tree are an important food source for wildlife and have long been appreciated by human palates as well. Pine nuts are a common ingredient in southwestern cuisine. *P. edulis* hybridizes with single-leaved pinyon pine *(P. monophylla),* producing a 2-leaved hybrid that is quite indistinguishable to novice naturalists but is the subject of great debate and investigation for taxonomists. **Where found:** hillsides, mountains, desert mountains and pinyon-juniper and foothill woodlands.

Monterey Cypress

Cupressus macrocarpa

Height: 80 ft
Leaves: evergreen, scale-like, ¾ in long
Seed cones: 1½ in long

Endemic to California's central coast, this tree is only naturalized in Southern California. The 2 small wild populations near Monterey and Carmel are of conservation concern because most of the original groves were destroyed for housing development and golf courses. • The Arizona cypress *(C. arizonica)* is a similar species that grows in the chaparral, foothill and pinyon-juniper woodlands of Southern California, reaching 50 ft tall; it also has many varieties that are popular in Southern Californian yards. • Monterey cypress on the coast grows sculptured and distorted by the ceaseless assault of wind and salt water that it endures throughout its 200- to 300-year lifespan. **Where found:** coastal sage scrub, chaparral. **Also known as:** macrocarpa (in New Zealand, where it is cultivated and grows up to 130 ft).

Incense Cedar

Calocedrus decurrens

Height: 60–80 ft, up to 150 ft in the Sierra Nevada
Needles: ⅛–½ in long, scale-like, overlapping
Seed cones: ¾–1½ in long

Although it is resistant to decay and thus is desirable for exterior building panels, incense cedar wood is most commonly used in the manufacture of pencils! If not fated to this studious enterprise, this tree is quite long lived—the oldest on record is 542 years old. • Incense cedar is a deciduous conifer, shedding its needles in fall. In dense groves, these trees can produce a couple of thousand pounds of litter per acre per year, providing ample fuel for many California forest fires. Studies show the natural fire cycle to be every 3–11 years. **Where found:** dry, shady sites in the mountain ranges.

Giant Sequoia

Sequoiadendron giganteum

Height: average 250 ft
Leaves: ⅛–½ in long, almost scale-like
Seed cones: 2–3½ in long

Giant sequoias are the world's largest trees in sheer volume, inspiring the largest tree-hugs around their bases. These trees can live 2000–3000 years, and the oldest known specimen dated by its stump rings was 3200 years old when it was cut. Living legends include the General Sherman in Sequoia National Park (the most massive at 52,500 ft³, with a trunk base of 109 ft in circumference) and the General Grant in Kings Canyon National Park (the tallest at 310 ft). **Where found:** yellow pine and redfir forests; botanical gardens and parks; about 75 groves are scattered along a 260-mi belt, nowhere more than about 15 mi wide, along the western slopes of the Sierra Nevada. **Also known as:** sequoia, bigtree, Sierra redwood.

Tanoak

Lithocarpus densiflorus

Height: 65–150 ft
Leaves: 4 in long, leathery, toothed margins
Flowers: 2–4 in long, upright catkins
Fruit: acorns with fringed cups, ¾–1¼ in long, ¾ in diameter

This tree was once classified in the *Quercus* genus but has now been given its own genus, *Lithocarpus*. It is believed to be an evolutionary link between the oaks (*Quercus* spp.) and chestnuts (*Castanea* spp.). The flowers resemble those of chestnuts but the fruit is an acorn, a characteristic of oaks. • This genus is typical of southeast Asia. • The leaves are leathery with toothed margins, evergreen and covered in hairs for the first few years. The bark is high in tannins and was used for tanning hides. **Where found:** montane, mainly in the Santa Ynez Mountains. **Also known as:** tanbark oak, California chestnut oak, chestnut oak, live oak, peach oak.

California Live Oak

Quercus agrifolia

Height: 30–80 ft
Leaves: 1–2¾ in long, ¾–1½ in wide,
spiny-toothed
Flowers: male in pendulous catkins,
2–4 in long; female inconspicuous
Fruit: ovoid acorns, 1–2½ in long,
½ in wide

The name "live oak" simply means that this oak is an evergreen, retaining green leaves and "living" through winter, though technically it is classified as a red oak. • The acorns of this oak were a staple for Native peoples. Charcoal made from the wood was used by the early Spaniards to fire their kilns to make adobe; in later years, the charcoal was used for gunpowder and electric power industries. • California live oak is the only oak that grows near the coast. **Where found:** valleys, slopes, mixed evergreen forests, and southern oak and foothill woodlands. **Also known as:** coast live oak.

Coastal Scrub Oak

Quercus dumosa

Height: up to 15 ft
Leaves: 1 in, evergreen, spiny margins
Flowers: small, ⅓–⅔ in wide, <⅓ in deep,
yellow or white
Fruit: acorn, <1 in

Inland oaks have so much variation that taxonomists have had a hard time determining species. There are at least 5 taxa in Southern California that until recently were all considered *Q. dumosa*. Popular perception of oaks places them in temperate zones of North America, but the greatest diversity of oak species exist in the montane forests of Mexico. **Where found:** desert margins, chaparall, coastal sage scrub, pinyon-juniper, Joshua tree and foothill woodlands, mixed forest and montane. **Also known as:** California scrub oak, Nuttall's scrub oak, inland scrub oak *(Q. berberidifolia),* Sonoran scrub oak *(Q. turbinella).*

Cottonwood

Populus fremontii

Height: 40–60 ft
Leaves: 1–3 in, deciduous, yellow in fall
Flowers: catkins, up to 6 in long, dioecious, female catkins are 3 times as long as male
Fruit: copious cottony seeds on female trees

Fast growing but not long lived, this tree is used for shade in livestock fields, and its wood is used for fuel and as a windbreak or streambank protection. • The young catkins and the sweet inner bark of spring were eaten by many Native peoples. Medicinally, the leaves, bark and resins from the sticky, aromatic buds were important for treating many conditions and ailments. The resins are still used today for salves, cough medicines and painkillers. • The abundant cottony seeds of the female plant create a lot of litter and apprehension in people with allergies. **Where found:** on moist to wet sites, often on shores; yellow pine and lodgepole forests, foothill woodlands, chaparral, valley grasslands and creosote bush scrub throughout Southern California.

Pacific Madrone

Arbutus menziesii

Height: 50–100 ft
Leaves: 2–6 in long
Flowers: ¼ in long, greenish white, sweet fragrance
Fruit: pea-sized, ¼ in across, persists on tree into winter

The Latin *Arbutus* and Spanish *madrone* translate to "strawberry tree," referring to the red fruits. • These trees are drought tolerant and are excellent cliff stabilizers because their long roots reach as far as the bedrock in search of water. • Medicinally, Pacific madrone was used traditionally to treat colds and stomach problems, as an astringent, as a tea to treat bladder infections, in sitz baths for other types of infections and as a postpartum contraceptive. **Where found:** foothill woodlands and montane; canyon and mountain slopes from sea level to 5000 ft.

159

Big-leaf Maple

Acer macrophyllum

Height: 50 ft
Leaves: 6–12 in across, 5-lobed
Flowers: ⅛ in across, greenish yellow, numerous,
in hanging clusters
Fruit: paired samaras, 1–2⅜ in long, wings in
a V-shape

Moss thrives on the big-leaf maple with such exuberance that the bark is often completely enrobed. The moss forms a thick layer in the tree's canopy, creating a "floating soil" into which other plants sprout and root. • The quantity and the sweetness of the sap from maples of the West do not match the famed maple syrup of their eastern counterparts. The leaves turn yellow or orange in fall. **Where found:** chaparral, foothill woodlands.

California Boxelder

Acer negundo var. *californicum*

Height: up to 50 ft
Leaves: 2–4 in long
Flowers: inconspicuous, male
and female on separate trees
Fruit: paired, 1–1½ in long,
V-shaped samaras

A subspecies of *A. negundo,* which is the most widely distributed North American maple, var. *californicum* is endemic to the state and is also a popular ornamental because of its colorful, shapely fruits and leaves. It resembles an ash and is the only North American species of maple with compound leaves. This tree grows quickly but is short-lived. Annual shoots can extend over 2 ft, but mature trees become brittle and burled and reach decadence at about 75 years of age. **Where found:** yellow pine forests, foothill woodlands and chaparral. **Also known as:** western boxelder, boxelder maple, maple ash.

California Laurel

Umbellularia californica

Height: usually 10–40 ft, but up to 80 ft
Leaves: 2–4 in long, evergreen, shiny yellow-green
Flowers: tiny yellow-green clusters of 6 to 10
Fruit: green drupes that mature to burgundy, 1 in long

The leaves of the laurel are a popular culinary seasoning better known as bay leaves. The aromatic menthol-like oil that can be derived from the foliage was also used medicinally in traditional medicine. The olive-like fruits and seeds are eaten by birds and small mammals such as squirrels. • The California laurel is one of the most preferred landscape specimens in gardens and parks owing to its glossy evergreen leaves, attractive fruit and slender crown. **Where found:** chaparral and foothill woodlands. **Also known as:** bay, bay laurel, California bay, myrtle.

Blue Palo Verde

Parkinsonia florida

Height: 15–20 ft tall and wide
Leaves: ½–1 in, bluish green, deciduous in cold and drought, short spines at the leaf nodes
Flowers: up to 1 in, pea-like, yellow
Fruit: seedpods 2–3 in long

Bluish green leaves and bark give the common name to this plant (the Spanish name meaning "green stick") and make it easy to identify, especially when it is in bloom with abundant yellow flowers that attract pollen-hungry bees. It is native to the Sonoran Desert, where it grows along desert washes; its deep penetrating root system helps it survive flash floods and reach low water tables during drought. • The Cahuilla Indians used to dry and grind the seeds into flour. **Where found:** desert washes, Sonoran Desert and creosote bush scrub. **Also known as:** *Cercidium floridum.*

161

California Fan Palm

Washingtonia filifera

Height: 30–60 ft
Leaves: blade up to 36 in, evergreen gray-green fronds
with stringy tips
Flowers: ⅜ in long in 12 in clusters, white
Fruit: oval, ½ in long

The dominant palm on Southern California's profile, this tree is a symbol of the famed sunny, freeze-free climate enjoyed here. This palm only grows in isolated groves in the wild but is in nearly every backyard and lining nearly every street in most cities and towns. The heavy wooden fronds are typically removed in urban settings, which is a labor-intensive job that is done by hand. If not removed, the fronds, or thatch, will fall in layers to create a sort of grass skirt around the trunk of the tree—excellent habitat for many animal species. **Where found:** creosote bush scrub.

Joshua Tree

Yucca brevifolia

Height: 3–20 ft
Leaves: 1–5 ft long
Flowers: large clusters of 1–2 in white
flowers on tall stalks;
inflorescence up to 5 in long
Fruit: leathery capsules, 1–4 in long

This species is the iconic and endemic tree of Joshua Tree National Forest, where it grows in impressive numbers; a similar subspecies, the Mohave yucca (*Y. schidigera*) grows elsewhere in Southern California. When the desert is in bloom in spring, the Joshua tree has impressive, large white flower clusters atop its crown of leaves. • Tree yuccas are very slow growing, taking decades to develop a distinctive tall trunk (when immature the crown grows close to the ground); many large specimens are dug up for transplanting in urban gardens, which has decimated some native populations. **Where found:** Joshua tree woodlands.

Eucalyptus

Eucalyptus globulus

Height: up to 180 ft
Leaves: 4–6 in long, waxy bluish green
Flowers: inconspicuous
Fruit: woody, ribbed, blue-gray spheres,
1 in wide, with a distinct rim

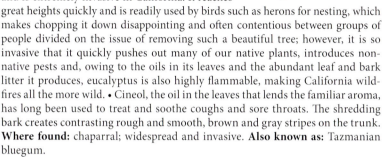

Though attractive and aromatic, this tree is native to Australia and is extremely invasive in California. It reaches great heights quickly and is readily used by birds such as herons for nesting, which makes chopping it down disappointing and often contentious between groups of people divided on the issue of removing such a beautiful tree; however, it is so invasive that it quickly pushes out many of our native plants, introduces non-native pests and, owing to the oils in its leaves and the abundant leaf and bark litter it produces, eucalyptus is also highly flammable, making California wildfires all the more wild. • Cineol, the oil in the leaves that lends the familiar aroma, has long been used to treat and soothe coughs and sore throats. The shredding bark creates contrasting rough and smooth, brown and gray stripes on the trunk. **Where found:** chaparral; widespread and invasive. **Also known as:** Tazmanian bluegum.

California Buckeye

Aesculus californica

Height: 15–30 ft
Leaves: palmately compound, 5 leaflets each 2–6 in long
Flowers: 1 in long, white to pale pink, sweet-scented, in erect clusters
Fruit: pear-like capsule, 2–3 in, containing a 1–2 in light brown to orange, poisonous seed

This tall shrub is beautiful and deadly. The bark, leaves and fruit contain the neurotoxic glycoside aesculin. Even the flower nectar is lethal to honey bees that have not co-evolved with this plant, and reportedly humans have been poisoned by eating honey with traces of California buckeye. Native peoples ingeniously used this plant to fish with by throwing meal made from ground buckeye seeds into pools of water. The toxins in the seed meal would stupefy the fish so they would loll about on the water's surface, where they were easily caught. **Where found:** chaparral, coastal sage scrub and foothill woodlands. **Also known as:** horsechestnut.

SHRUBS

Shrubs survive several seasons and are therefore perennials. They have one or more woody stems or can be a vine, and they are normally less than 16 ft tall. Shrubs usually produce flowers and fruit. They provide habitat and shelter for a variety of animals, and their berries, leaves and often bark are crucial sources of food for many animals. The tasty berries of some shrubs have been a staple of Native and traditional foods, and they are still enjoyed by people everywhere.

Junipers
p. 166

Heaths
p. 166

Willows
pp. 167–68

Dogwoods
p. 168

Roses
pp. 169–72

Peas
p. 172

Asters
p. 173

California Lilac
p. 174

Honeysuckles
pp. 174–75

Almond/Cashew
pp. 175–76

Creeping Barberry
p. 176

Creosote Bush
p. 177

California Flannel Bush
p. 177

Junipers

Juniperus spp.

Height: shrubs of a few ft to tree forms of several ft
Needles: ¼–¾ in long, sometimes scale-like
Seed cones: about ½ in long

Blue-gray juniper "berries" are, in fact, tiny cones with fleshy scales. They can add spice to food and flavoring to gin, but pregnant women and people with kidney problems should never use them. They can be toxic in large quantities. • Europeans made juniper berry tea to treat eating disorders, diarrhea and heart, lung and kidney problems. Native peoples burned branches of this pungently aromatic evergreen to purify homes, protect people from evil and bring good luck to hunters. **Where found:** pinyon-juniper and Joshua tree woodlands; dry, open sites in plains to alpine zones.

Prince's-pine

Chimaphila umbellata

Height: 4–12 in
Leaves: ¾–3 in, whorled, evergreen
Flowers: <½ in long, pink, waxy
Fruit: round capsules, ¼ in across

Prince's-pine has been used to flavor candy, soft drinks (especially root beer) and traditional beers. The leaves of this semi-woody, evergreen shrub are glossy and dark green above and pale beneath. • Native peoples used a tea made from this plant as a remedy for fluid retention, kidney or bladder problems, fevers and coughs. Several Native groups smoked the dried leaves. • These attractive plants need certain soil fungi to live, so they usually die when transplanted. They are best enjoyed in the wild. **Where found:** foothill woodlands (usually coniferous) and montane. **Also known as:** pipsissewa.

Common Bearberry

Arctostaphylos uva-ursi

Height: 2–6 in
Leaves: ½–1¼ in long, leathery
Flowers: ⅛–¼ in long, pinkish white, urn-shaped
Fruit: berry-like drupes, ¼–½ in across, bright red

Thick, leathery evergreen leaves help this common, mat-forming shrub survive on dry, sunny slopes where others would perish. • The "berries" are edible but are rather mealy and tasteless. Native groups cooked them and mixed them with grease or fish eggs to reduce their dryness. The glossy leaves were widely used for smoking, both alone and later with tobacco. • The long, trailing branches send down roots, and the flowers nod in small clusters. **Where found:** coastal sage scrub; well-drained, open or wooded sites from foothills to alpine zones in the western portion of the state. **Also known as:** kinnikinnick.

Manzanita

Arctostaphylos spp.

Height: 6–20 ft
Leaves: ¾–2 in, evergreen, leathery
Flowers: ¼ in long, white or pink, bell-shaped, drooping, in clusters
Fruit: berry-like drupes, ⅓–½ in, white maturing to deep red

Manzanitas are characterized by smooth orange or red bark and stiff, twisting branches.

• An important member of the chaparral, this evergreen shrub is poor browsing for livestock but a valuable food source for wildlife such as coyotes, foxes and various bird species, especially grouse, which eat the fruits. • The word *manzanita* is Spanish for "little apple." **Where found:** coastal sage scrub, chaparral, montane, foothill and Joshua tree woodlands, dry slopes, hillsides and canyons; widespread.

Scouler's Willow

Salix scouleriana

Height: 6½–30 ft
Leaves: 1¼–4 in long
Flowers: ¾–1⅝ in long catkins
Fruit: silky reddish brown capsules, ¼–⅜ in long

Willows are extremely common, but it is often difficult to identify each species. Dense, elongating flower clusters (catkins) and buds covered by a single scale identify this group. • Scouler's willow is a spindly, clumped, deciduous shrub with short, stiff, rust-colored hairs on the undersides of its leaves. The seed (female) catkins appear before the leaves and produce long-beaked, short-stalked, hairy capsules containing tiny, silky-tufted seeds. • Sitka willow (*S. sitchensis*) grows 3–26 ft tall, with brittle twigs, silky capsules and catkins 2–3 in long that often appear before the leaves in spring. **Where found:** yellow pine, lodgepole and subalpine forests, foothill woodlands, chaparral, valley grasslands, wetland-riparian areas and montane. **Also known as:** Nuttall's willow.

Desert Willow

Chilopsis linearis

Height: 10–25 ft
Leaves: 14 in
Flowers: clusters of 1–1½ in
long pink blossoms
Fruit: seedpods, 4–12 in

This fast-growing plant with clusters of pink flowers has become a popular shrub in domestic gardens, and cultivars exist with flowers that range in color from pink to dark purple or burgundy to white. Well adapted to the desert and commonly found in the Mohave and Sonoran, it is extremely drought tolerant in contrast to true willows that are riparian. "Willow" in the common name refers to the shrub's willow-like deciduous leaves. **Where found:** coastal bush scrub, Joshua-tree woodlands, deserts and canyons in sandy soils and desert washes and flats.

Red-osier Dogwood

Cornus sericea

Height: 1½–10 ft
Leaves: ¾–4 in long, prominently veined
Flowers: <¼ in wide, white,
in dense clusters
Fruit: berry-like drupes, about ¼ in wide

This attractive, hardy, deciduous shrub has distinctive purple to red branches with white flowers in spring, red leaves in fall and white "berries" in winter. It is easily grown from cuttings. • Native peoples smoked the dried inner bark alone or with tobacco or common bearberry (kinnikinnick). The flexible branches were often woven into baskets, especially as decorative red rims. The bitter, juicy berries, mixed with sweeter fruit or sugar, made a "sweet-and-sour" treat. **Where found:** chaparral, foothill woodlands and montane.

Western Serviceberry

Amelanchier alnifolia

Height: 3½–16 ft
Leaves: ¾–2 in long
Flowers: ¾ in wide, 5-petaled showy white flowers in clusters (racemes)
Fruit: roundish green berries that mature to dark purple in early summer, ¼–½ in wide

The pretty, slightly fragrant white flowers on twisting ornate branches of gray or brown bark were apparently popular for decorating country churches, hence the common name. More popular is the sweet blueberry-like fruit, made into jams, jellies and pies. • This far ranging genus is known in Canada as saskatoonberry; in Southern California, the western and Utah serviceberries *(A. utahensis),* found in lower, drier habitats, are most common. • In fall, the leaves turn attractive shades of yellow, orange and red. **Where found:** foothill woodlands.

Mountain Mahogany

Cercocarpus montanus

Height: 5–15 ft
Leaves: 1 in
Flowers: small, non-showy white
Fruit: feathery heads, 1–3 in long

In fall, the leaves of the mountain mahogany become almost obscured by a proliferation of long, wispy, twisting tails of white feathery seeds. • Deer, bighorn sheep, elk and pronghorn as well as domestic sheep and cattle forage on the nearly evergreen leaves, which are silvery white underneath, inspiring a secondary common name. • This member of the rose family is adapted to tolerate the fire regime of regeneration in Southern California. **Where found:** chaparral, montane and pinyon-juniper and foothill woodlands. **Also known as:** *C. betuloides*; silverleaf mountain mahogany.

Island Ironwood Tree

Lyonothamnus floribundus asplenifolius

Height: 20–50 ft
Leaves: 4–6 in, lobed with fern-like leaflets
Flowers: 4–8 in wide, white clusters
Fruit: woody capsule, ¼ in, contains two pairs of seeds

A pretty plant with glossy fern-like leaves, shredding red-brown bark and dense clusters of flowers, island ironwood tree is native to the Channel Islands, but because of its ornate qualities, it has been introduced to the mainland and into people's gardens. As with many island species, this endemic plant is rare and endangered, and careful island management is required to protect it and other island plants and animals from hybridizing with mainland forms. **Where found:** chaparral, foothill woodlands, coastal slopes, hills and canyons; native to the Channel and Catalina islands and naturalized to the mainland coast of Los Angeles and Santa Barbara counties.

Toyon

Heteromeles arbutifolia

Height: 6–15 ft, spreading 4–5 ft
Leaves: 2–4 in, evergreen, leathery
Flowers: ¼ in white flowers in showy clusters
Fruit: red pomes, ¼ in

Beautiful at any time of year for its lovely white flowers, its striking red fruits or its dense evergreen foliage, this plant is becoming a popular native landscape plant in urban gardens, but it is an important species for wildlife as well. Butterflies and bees feed on the flowers, and birds and small mammals rely on its fruit in winter. The bright red fruits are reminiscent of holly. **Where found:** foothill woodlands, coastal sage scrub, chaparral and montane. **Also known as:** Christmas berry.

Thimbleberry

Rubus parviflorus

Height: 1½–6½ ft
Leaves: 2–8 in wide, 3–7-lobed, similar to a maple leaf
Flowers: 1–2 in wide, white
Fruit: raspberry-like, red, ⅝–¾ in wide

This plant's beautiful, satiny berries are seedy and difficult to collect, but most Native peoples ate them fresh from the bush because they are so common. Thimbleberries can be tasteless, tart or sweet, depending on the season and the site, but birds and bears always seem to enjoy them. • Native peoples also ate the young shoots, and the broad leaves provided temporary plates, containers and basket liners. • This deciduous shrub, without prickles, often forms dense thickets. **Where found:** yellow pine or mixed evergreen forests and moist to dry sites in foothill woodlands and montane throughout most of Southern California.

Ninebark

Physocarpus capitatus

Height: 12 ft
Leaves: 1½–3½ in wide, 1⅛–2⅜ in long, 3–5-lobed
Flowers: ½ in long, white, 5 petals, in rounded clusters
Fruit: reddish brown follicles, ¼ in long, in dense, upright clusters

Although it is slightly toxic, many Native peoples used this plant medicinally, following the old adage that "what doesn't kill you, cures you." • This shrub is named for the supposed 9 layers of bark that can be peeled away from the stem. • The leaves turn to intense reds and oranges in fall. **Where found:** low to mid elevations in wet, somewhat open places such as thickets along streams and lakes, coastal marshes and edges of moist woodlands, chaparral, yellow pine forests and wetland-riparian areas; native to the Sierra Nevada.

Oceanspray

Holodiscus discolor

Height: up to 10 ft
Leaves: ¾–2½ in long, hairy
Flowers: tiny, creamy white, in dense clusters 4–7 in long
Fruit: tiny, light brown, in large clusters that persist through winter

As its name attests, this species is very tolerant of salt spray and maritime conditions, though it is also common inland on the western slopes of the Cascade Mountains. Its hardiness makes it a pioneer species on disturbed sites. • Imaginative minds have drawn comparison between the drooping clusters of tiny white flowers and frothy sea foam dripping from the shrubs hanging over coastal cliff sides. **Where found:** forest edges, cliff edges and coastlines in coastal to low montane zones. **Also known as:** creambush.

Shrubby Cinquefoil

Dasiphora floribunda

Height: 1–4 ft
Leaves: compound, leaflets ½–¾ in long, grayish green
Flowers: ¾ in, yellow, 5 petals
Fruit: achenes, ⅝–1¼ in wide, light brown, hairy

This hardy deciduous shrub is sometimes seen in gardens and public places. It is often covered with bright yellow blooms from spring to fall. Shrubby cinquefoil also provides erosion control, especially along highways. • Heavily browsed cinquefoils indicate overgrazing, because most animals prefer other plants. • Native peoples used the papery, shredding bark as tinder for fires. **Where found:** various habitats, wet to dry, often rocky sites from plains to subalpine zones; throughout most of Southern California. **Also known as:** *Potentilla fruticosa*; *Pentaphylloides floribunda*.

Bitterbrush

Purshia tridentata

Height: to 8 ft
Leaves: 1 in long
Flowers: ⅝ in long, cream-colored, tubular, solitary
Fruit: about ⅝ in long, spindle-shaped, seed-like

Bitterbrush has very similar leaves to sagebrush (though they are not aromatic), but it has small, bright yellow, rose-like flowers and velvety, seed-like fruits. It is an abundant shrub and an important member of the sagebrush community in dry parts of the state. Its hardiness and abundance makes this plant important forage for deer and elk, and the abundant yellow flowers add splashes of color to the dry landscape. **Where found:** coastal sage scrub, creosote bush scrub and desert. **Also known as:** antelopebrush.

Chamise

Adenostoma fasciculatum

Height: to 2–12 ft
Leaves: ¼–½ in long, sharply pointed
Flowers: ⅕ in small, white, 5 petals, in clusters 1½–5 in long at branch ends
Fruit: inconspicuous dry achenes

This California native is one of the most widespread and characteristic shrubs of the chaparral, forming dense stands called chamissal. Chamise is an important ground cover that prevents soil desiccation and wind erosion. • An evergreen of the rose family, this plant has 5-petaled, white flowers that turn rusty with age. • Flammable oils in the shiny leaves cause intense, dramatic wildfires, a necessary cycle to clear the dry vegetation and encourage fresh regrowth. Chamise roots and crowns survive the fire, holding the soil and soon regenerating. **Where found:** chaparral. **Also known as:** greasewood.

Scotch Broom

Cytisus scoparius

Height: 6–8 ft
Leaves: ½–1 in long, divided into 3 leaflets
Flowers: ¾–1 in long, yellow
Fruit: flattened, black pods, 1–1½ in long

Bright masses of golden yellow flowers fill hedges, ditches and roadsides with radiant color, though Scotch broom is not regarded with much pleasure by botanists. This shrub is classified as a noxious weed. An invasive, introduced species from Europe, it is amazingly prolific and spreads rapidly over wide areas. Reportedly, 3 seeds planted on Vancouver Island, Canada, in 1850, subsequently colonized the entire island. **Where found:** invades natural meadows, open forests and disturbed sites at low elevations.

Desert Ironwood

Olneya tesota

Height: 15–30 ft up to 45 ft
Leaves: 2 in, with ¾ in leaflets, pair of ½ in thorns at base
Flowers: ¼ in pea-like lavender flowers in clusters
Fruit: seedpods, 2 in, with 1–4 shiny brown seeds

Evergreen bluish gray leaves and demure lavender flowers on winding gray branches give this desert shrub a whimsical look. The wood is among the densest in the world, hence the plant's common name. This hardy shrub is an oasis in the harsh Sonoran Desert, where wildlife relies on it for food (eating the seeds), shade and nesting cavities; legumes grow in the leaf litter, and other plants grow within the complex of its several trunks. Capable of surviving 800 years, it is one of the longest-living Sonoran plants. **Where found:** creosote bush scrub and dry ephemeral washes of the Sonoran Desert.

Coyote Brush

Baccharis pilularis

Height: up to 12 ft
Leaves: ½–1½ in evergreen
Flowers: 1–2 in, white male and female flowers
Fruit: achene, ¹⁄₁₆–¹⁄₃₂ in, with tawny hairy bristles (pappus) to ½ in long

Coyote brush is a member of the aster family. Its flowering heads turn to fuzzy achenes similar to a dandelion. It is shade intolerant and is replaced by other plants in mature chaparral and creosote sage communities, but is a dominant species after a fire and is one of the first plants to colonize burned areas. Coyote brush is an important source of cover and forage species for rabbits and small rodents. **Where found:** coastal sage scrub, chaparral, hillsides and canyons. **Also known as:** chaparral broom.

Sagebrush

Artemisia tridentata

Height: 1½–6½ ft
Leaves: ½–¾ in long, silvery, 3 teeth at the tip
Flowers: very small, yellow, in heads ½–2¾ in wide
Fruit: tiny achenes

This plant is not a true sage, but rather a species of aster. • This common shrub, with a pungent, sage-like aroma and grayish, shredding bark, has been used in a wide variety of medicines and was also burned as a smudge and fumigant. • Sagebrush is a valuable food for many wild birds and mammals, but livestock avoid it. Early settlers knew that its presence indicated groundwater. **Where found:** coastal sage scrub and pinyon-juniper woodlands; often covers many acres of dry plains and slopes. **Also known as:** common sagebrush, mountain sagebrush, big sagebrush.

Rabbitbush

Chrysothamnus nauseosus

Height: 8–24 in
Leaves: 1¼–2½ in long, narrow, gray-green, velvety
Flowers: ¼ in wide, yellow, in dense clusters
Fruit: tufted achenes, ⅕ in

In late summer, this flat-topped, deciduous shrub covers dry slopes with splashes of yellow. A hardy species, this plant thrives on poor soils and in harsh conditions. • Native peoples made medicinal teas from the roots or leaves to treat coughs, colds, fevers and menstrual pain. The dense branches were used to cover and carpet sweathouses, and they were burned slowly to smoke hides. Boiled flowerheads produced a lemon yellow dye for wool, leather and baskets. **Where found:** Joshua tree and pinyon-juniper woodlands; dry, open areas in plains, foothills and montane. **Also known as:** rubber rabbitbrush.

California Lilacs

Ceanothus spp.

Height: 4–25 ft
Leaves: to 2 in long, glossy
Flowers: tiny, white or blue, in plumes 2–6 in long
Fruit: dry capsules, each with a ⅕ in hard seed

This genus, known collectively as the California lilacs, has widespread species from Canada to Guatemala but almost all are found in California. In Southern California there are at least 16 native species. The plumes of fragrant flowers vary from white to blue to lilac in color, depending on the species, but these color variations also exist within some single species. **Where found:** widespread in chaparral, foothills, Joshua tree and pinyon-juniper woodlands and coastal sage scrub.

Common Snowberry

Symphoricarpos albus

Height: 1½–2½ ft
Leaves: >¾–1⅝ in
Flowers: ⅛–⅓ in, pinkish, in clusters
Fruit: white berries, ¼–½ in

The name "snowberry" refers to the waxy, white, berry-like drupes that remain in small clusters near branch tips through winter. All parts of these deciduous shrubs are toxic, causing vomiting and diarrhea. Some Native peoples called the fruits "corpse berries," because they were believed to be the ghosts of saskatoons—part of the spirit world, not to be eaten by the living. The broadly funnel-shaped flowers are pink to white and have hairy centers. **Where found:** mixed evergreen, yellow pine and foothill woodlands, streambanks, canyons and occasionally in wetlands.

Twinberry

Lonicera involucrata

Height: 3½–6½ ft
Leaves: 2–6 in long
Flowers: ½–¾ in long, yellow, tubular
Fruit: black berries, <⅜ in across, in pairs

The unusual, shiny berries of these deciduous shrubs, with their broad, spreading, backward-bending, shiny red to purplish bracts, catch the eyes of passersby and also of hungry bears and birds. Despite their tempting appearance, these berries are bitter and unpalatable to humans, and they can be toxic. **Where found:** moist to wet, usually shaded sites in foothills, montane and subalpine zones. **Also known as:** bracted honeysuckle, crowberry.

Elderberry

Sambucus spp.

Height: 3–20 ft
Leaves: compound,
5–7 leaflets each
2–6 in
Flowers: ⅛–¼ in wide,
whitish, in clusters
Fruit: berry-like drupes, ¼ in,
red, blue or black

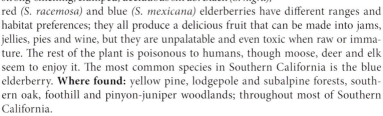

Large, showy clusters of flowers or heavy, wide "berries" draw attention to this strong-smelling, clumped, deciduous shrub. Black *(S. nigra),* red *(S. racemosa)* and blue *(S. mexicana)* elderberries have different ranges and habitat preferences; they all produce a delicious fruit that can be made into jams, jellies, pies and wine, but they are unpalatable and even toxic when raw or immature. The rest of the plant is poisonous to humans, though moose, deer and elk seem to enjoy it. The most common species in Southern California is the blue elderberry. **Where found:** yellow pine, lodgepole and subalpine forests, southern oak, foothill and pinyon-juniper woodlands; throughout most of Southern California.

Poison Oak

Toxicodendron diversilobum

Height: 3–7 ft, sometimes vining up to 50 ft
Leaves: 3–5 irregular lobes (similar to an oak leaf), 1–2 in long
Flowers: tiny, yellow, 5 petals, in loose racemes
Fruit: berries, ¼ in across, white or cream-colored

Poison oak is not an oak, and poison ivy is not an ivy—both are members of the sumac family (Anacardiaceae) and contain the potent allergen urushiol. This substance can stay active on unwashed clothing or on cut branches for up to a year, and smoke from burning branches can damage lung, nose and throat tissues. Not everyone is affected, but some people contract a painful, red, long-lasting rash. Avoid this plant by remembering the rhyme "Leaves of 3, let it be." • The leaves turn bright scarlet in fall. **Where found:** yellow pine forests, foothill woodlands, chaparral and valley grasslands; widespread along the Pacific Coast from Canada to Baja California.

Skunkbrush

Rhus trilobata

Height: 2–12 ft tall and wide
Leaves: 3 leaflets, 2–3 in long
Flowers: inconspicuous, white to yellowish clusters
Fruit: hard red drupes, ¼ in

The deciduous 3-lobed leaves turn red and orange in fall. In spring, the clusters of yellowish flowers blossom before the leaves appear. • This plant has a pungent medicinal aroma that is disagreeable enough to those with a sensitive sense of smell to have been given the name skunkbrush. It has traditional medicinal uses in treating cold symptoms (with a tea made from the bark) or tooth- and stomach-aches (with the berries, which are sour but edible and make a tart, refreshing drink similar to lemonade). **Where found:** canyons, shrublands, creosote bush scrub, chaparral, pinyon-juniper and foothill woodlands. **Also known as:** sourberry, squaw bush, three-leaf sumac

Creeping Barberry

Mahonia aquifolium

Height: 4–6 ft
Leaves: 6–12 in long, divided into 5–9 spiny leaflets, each 2–3 in long
Flowers: tiny, yellow, bell-shaped, in clusters 1–2½ in across
Fruit: bluish berry, ½ in

This shrub does not drop its leaves in winter, but calling it evergreen is a misnomer because the leaves turn a glorious red color; they are popular in Christmas plant arrangements and decorative accents. • The juicy berries are sour but edible, and herbalists used to make a tincture from the bright yellow roots to treat digestive disorders. *M. repens* also grows here and is almost indistinguishable from *M. aquifolium*. **Where found:** streambanks, shaded slopes, chaparral and coniferous forests.

Creosote Bush

Larrea tridentata

Height: 3–6 ft
Leaves: ⅜ in, evergreen, resinous
Flowers: ½ in, yellow
Fruit: dry reddish capsule containing 5–10 ⅓-in fuzzy seeds

In the Mojave and Sonoran deserts, in the hottest driest conditions, creosote bush thrives and is the dominant species in the landscape zone that shares its name—the creosote bush scrub. It clones itself by suckering and therefore spreads underground, escaping fires and allowing an individual plant to perpetually survive in the guise of subsequent generations (one individual in the Mojave known as the King Clone is estimated to be 11,700 years old). • On the rare occasions of rainfall, the plant becomes aromatic, lending a fresh perfume to the desert. • It is an important shelter plant for many species of desert reptiles. **Where found:** creosote bush scrub in the Mojave and Sonoran deserts.

California Flannel Bush

Fremontodendron californicum

Height: 5–20 ft, up to twice as wide
Leaves: ½–2 in, 3–5 lobed evergreen
Flowers: 1½–3 in, yellow
Fruit: capsule, ¾–1 in

An impressive plant of the chaparral, California flannel bush gets its name from the dense covering of fine hairs on its leaves. In spring, this plant produces an abundance of yellow flowers, adding even more bright color to its sunny environment. Entire hillsides may be covered with this shrub, and when it is in bloom, the color lays over the landscape like a great yellow flannel blanket. **Where found:** foothill and pinyon-juniper woodlands.

HERBS, FERNS, CACTI, SUCCULENTS & SEAWEEDS

The plants in this section are all non-woody plants and include herbs, ferns, cacti, succulents and seaweeds. Herbs can be annual, though many are perennial, growing from a persistent rootstock. Most of those with flowering stems later produce fruit. Various forms of seeds are familiar, such as those of the sunflower and the white parachute seeds of the dandelion. Many of these plants can be used for adding flavor to foods, and in medicine, aromatherapy and dyes. The many unique flowers are an inspiration to artists and poets and are often symbols of romance, or have special meaning in folklore, legend or superstition.

Ferns are prehistoric plants with large, lacy leaves commonly called fronds. Certain types of fern, such as fiddleheads, are appreciated for their delicious flavor. In the wild, ferns are an important groundcover and are associated with microrrhyzal fungi. They are being studied for their ability to remove heavy metals, particularly arsenic, from soil.

Cacti and succulents have long been prized by Native peoples as a source of food and water in the harsh desert climate. When the first European botanists came onto the scene, they applied the name *kaktos* (Greek for "thistle") to these plants. In recent years, collectors around the world have been selling desert plants in souvenir shops and nurseries, and many species have become threatened or endangered because of over-collecting. Fortunately, most are now propagated from seeds and cuttings. Cacti and succulents have many impressive adaptations to prevent water loss, such as leaves modified into thorns and a waxy or furry epidermis. These plants transpire 6000 times less than ordinary plants.

Seaweeds are algae and can be classified into 3 major groups: green, red and brown. They absorb all the required fluids, nutrients and gases directly from the water and, unlike terrestrial plants, do not require an inner system for conducting fluids and nutrients. However, seaweeds do contain chlorophyll to absorb the sunlight needed for photosynthesis. They also contain other light-absorbing pigments.

Lilies
p. 180

Miner's Lettuce
p. 180

Field Chickweed
p. 181

Mustards
p. 181–82

Poppies & Bleeding Hearts
p. 182–83

Saxifrages
pp. 182–83

Buttercups
pp. 184–85

Roses
p. 186

Violets
p. 186

Peas
p. 187

Fireweed
p. 188

Cow Parsnip
p. 188

Gentian
p. 189

Waterleaf
pp. 189–90

Phlox
p. 190

Downingia
p. 190

Pennyroyal
p. 191

Snapdragons
pp. 192–93

Asters
pp. 193–95

Sulphur Buckwheat
p. 195

Ferns
p. 196

Desert Agave
p. 197

Cacti
p. 197

Winterfat
p. 197

Seaweeds & Algae
pp. 198–99

California False-Hellebore

Veratrum californicum

Height: 3–5 ft
Leaves: 6–16 in long, 2–6 in wide
Flowers: 1 in wide, white to greenish, star-like, in terminal clusters
Fruit: egg-shaped capsules, ¾–1⅛ in long

Alternating, corn-like leaves give this plant one of its common names, corn lily, but it is by no means edible. False-hellebores are members of a very poisonous group of plants. A similar species, green false-hellebore (*V. viride*) is one of the most poisonous plants in the Pacific Northwest. When livestock eat this plant, it causes severe deformities in their offspring, particularly in sheep. **Where found:** damp or wet areas of the mountains. **Also known as:** corn lily.

Death Camas

Zigadenus spp.

Height: 18–23 in
Leaves: up to 12 in long
Flowers: tiny, white, in clusters
Fruit: 3-lobed capsules, ¾ in long

Deadly poisonous, the bulbs of this plant look similar to those of the blue- or purple-flowered edible camas (*Camassia* spp.), which was an important food staple to Native peoples and often grows alongside death camas. The edible variety is easily identifiable by the flowers (blue to purple vs. white). • This plant is notorious for poisoning sheep and occasionally other livestock, but well-fed animals usually avoid it. Ingestion results in convulsions, coma and then death. **Where found:** coastal sage scrub, foothill woodlands, chaparral, valley grasslands, open yellow pine or mixed evergreen forests, wetland-riparian areas and rocky or grassy slopes, at low to mid elevations. **Also known as:** star lily.

Miner's Lettuce

Claytonia perfoliata

Height: 1–16 in
Leaves: up to 4 in wide, 2 stem leaves usually fused into a disk
Flowers: ⅛–¼ in wide, numerous (5–40), white or pinkish
Fruit: 3-segmented capsules, about ⅕ in, containing 3 tiny black seeds

Remarkably fleshy, succulent leaves make this species easily distinguishable. The juicy basal leaves completely encircle the stem to showcase the tiny, delicate flowers. • This plant's common name comes from the fact that early settlers (and miners) collected this plant for salads. **Where found:** moist open to shady sites, chaparral, forests, thickets, meadows and disturbed sites, often in sandy soils, at low to mid elevations (below 6000 ft). **Also known as:** *Montia perfoliata*.

Field Chickweed

Cerastium arvense

Height: 2–12 in
Leaves: ½–1¼ in long, narrow
Flowers: ⅛–½ in wide, white, in open, flat-topped clusters
Fruit: long capsules, 2–3½ in

Aptly named, chickweed was fed to chickens, goslings and caged birds, especially when the birds were ill. • The genus name *Cerastium* comes from the Greek *kerastes*, "horned," in reference to the curved, cylindrical capsules, which open by 10 small teeth at the tip. The leaves of this loosely clumped perennial often have secondary leafy tufts in their axils. **Where found:** chaparral and dry, open, often rocky sites in plains to alpine zones.

American Winter Cress

Barbarea orthoceras

Height: ½–2 ft
Leaves: to 4½ in long, becoming simpler and smaller higher up the stem
Flowers: ½ in long, yellow, 4-petaled, clustered in a raceme
Fruit: seedpods (siliques), to 2 in long

This biennial herb grows fairly tall and erect from its woody base and explodes in bright yellow flower clusters. The leaves are interesting and distinctive, with 2–3 pairs of smaller lobes and 1 large lobe. **Where found:** meadows, streambanks, beaches and moist to wet forests and openings at low to mid elevations.

Field Mustard

Brassica rapa

Height: 1–6 ft
Leaves: up to 12 in long, lobed, becoming simpler and smaller higher up the stem
Flowers: yellow, 4 petals, ½ in wide
Fruit: narrow pods, 1–2 in long

Golden fields of mustard are a beautiful sight and are often one of the first splashes of color to announce the arrival of spring. • Although there are many genera in the mustard family, the *Brassica* are the ones that most commonly come to mind. A member of a group of cultivated plants, *Brassica* is Latin for "cabbage," and *rapa* means "turnip." The word "mustard" appears to derive from the Latin *mustum* for "new wine," which was the first pressing of the grapes and was mixed with crushed mustard seeds to make a sauce. **Where found:** chaparral and agricultural areas below 4000 ft. **Also known as:** rapeseed; *B. campestris*.

Milk Maids

Cardamine californica

Height: 1½–2 ft
Leaves: ½–2¾ in long, rounded
Flowers: ½–¾ in wide, 4 petals
Fruit: seedpod, up to 2 in long

One of the first to flower in spring, this plant has pale pink or white flowers that are commonly seen in shady canyons, on foothill slopes, in woodlands and in shady gardens, often early in the new year. In wet areas, it can grow in exuberant masses. **Where found:** chaparral, shady canyons and woodlands below 3500 ft. **Also known as:** toothwort; *Dentaria californica*.

Peppergrass

Lepidium nitidum

Height: 4–16 in
Leaves: alternate, up to 4 in at the base but becoming smaller higher up the stem
Flowers: ¼ in across
Fruit: oval seedpod, ¼ in long

Many mustards are more noticeable for their seedpods than for their flowers, and peppergrass is no exception. When the tiny, white flowers go to seed, they drop their petals, and the seedpods mature from green to a gorgeous reddish purple. The seedpods give this species its common name because they are shiny and peppery-tasting. **Where found:** chaparral, deserts and in large patches on dry flats, grassy slopes and disturbed sites below 3000 ft.

California Poppy

Eschscholzia californica

Height: 2–24 in
Leaves: tiny, mostly basal, highly divided (parsley-like)
Flowers: to 2 in wide, solitary, yellow to orange, 4 petals
Fruit: pod-like capsules of tiny black or dark brown seeds, 1–3½ in

The state flower of California, this bright, showy species sets fields and slopes ablaze with orange and gold. There are many varieties of California poppy, but the flowers all have a distinctive pink pedestal, like a platter, with the bloom showcased atop. This plant is more noticeable once the leaves fall and only the fat, dry seedpods remain. **Where found:** chaparral, deserts, dry rocky slopes and disturbed sites such as roadsides and clearings at low elevations.

Pacific Bleeding Heart

Dicentra formosa

Height: 6–20 in
Leaves: 12 in long, basal, fern-like
Flowers: ¾–1 in long, pink-purple, heart-shaped
Fruit: oblong capsules, ⅓–¾ in long

Pacific bleeding heart is native to North America and Asia. • The common name refers to the heart-shaped flower, which ranges in color from light pink to intense deep purple or magenta. This plant is also cultivated and highly hybridized in color and size for gardens. • Though this bleeding heart is also found in the dry chaparral, its soft, leafy, fern-like foliage is one of the common lush, green groundcovers in shady, moist forests. **Where found:** chaparral, forests and moist sites along ravines and streambanks at low to mid elevations. **Also known as:** western bleeding heart.

Small-flowered Woodland Star

Lithophragma parviflorum

Height: 1–3 ft
Leaves: 1–2 in, 3-lobed, basal
Flowers: ½ in across, white to pink, 4–14 alternately arranged up the stem
Fruit: 3-chambered capsules, up to ⅓ in long

When caught up in a breeze, these star-like flowers atop their slender stems sway like magic wands conducting spells across the meadows. The white, pink or lavender flowers have 5 petals, each with 3 lobes, and are closely attached to the stems. • This flower makes its appearance in spring on wooded foothills where, typical of the saxifrage family, it finds its preferred rocky habitat. **Where found:** grassy slopes, open areas with rocky soil, dry forests and coastal bluffs at low to mid elevations throughout most of Southern California.

Brook Saxifrage

Saxifraga odontoloma

Height: ½–1½ ft
Leaves: up to 8 in long, basal, toothed
Flowers: ¼ in across, 5 petals
Fruit: capsules, ¼ in long

Saxifrage means "stone breaker," referring the preference of some species for rocky habitats such as mountain ridges or even stone walls. • Brook saxifrage displays all the characteristics of a typical saxifrage: a leafless stem rising above large, round, basal, scallop-toothed leaves and many gracefully hanging flowers with spade-shaped white petals and contrasting yellow dots. **Where found:** streambanks, lodgepole and subalpine forests, and wetland-riparian areas in the southeastern portion of the state, namely San Bernardino County.

Pacific Sedum

Sedum spathulifolium

Height: 2–12 in
Leaves: ¾ in long, ⅜ in wide, basal
Flowers: ⅜ in long, yellow, in flat-topped clusters
Fruit: erect follicles in 5 segments

Stonecrops are noted for their distinctive succulent leaves, a strategy to conserve water in dry habitats. Pacific sedum has crowded, wedge-shaped leaves that alternate to form a basal rosette. These delicate leaves turn reddish if exposed to full sunshine; however, they remain green long after being picked, giving them the colloquial name of "livelong." **Where found:** chaparral, shady to partially shady rocky sites or coarse soils, mountain cliffs, coastal bluffs and forest openings at low to mid elevations. **Also known as:** Pacific stonecrop, broad-leaved stonecrop.

Windflower

Anemone drummondii

Height: 4–10 in
Leaves: ¾–2 in long
Flowers: 1–1½ in wide
Fruit: achenes, <1 inch long, in clusters

A burst of yellow stamens and 5–8 white or bluish sepals are the showy parts of this flower, which doesn't actually have true petals. After the flowers fade, the woolly, spherical fruits catch our interest, looking like wind-tousled heads and giving the plant its common name as well as the genus name *Anemone*, which means "shaken in the wind." • This plant thrives in windy, high-alpine conditions. **Where found:** rocky slopes in mid to high elevations; yellow pine, lodgepole and subalpine forests. **Also known as:** Drummond's anemone, alpine anemone.

Western Columbine

Aquilegia formosa

Height: 1–4 ft
Leaves: variable, usually twice divided into 3s, ⅜–2 in long
Flowers: 1–1½ in long, tubular, red and yellow with reddish spurs
Fruit: 5 erect ½–1 in follicles with hairy, spreading tips

This plant's colorful flowers entice hummingbirds, butterflies and people to sip their sweet nectar, though the latter do a poor job at pollinating. The entire flower is edible and is decorative in salads. **Where found:** chaparral, pinyon-juniper woodlands, open to partly shady meadows, forest openings, clearings, rocky slopes, beaches and montane from low elevation to treeline. **Also known as:** crimson columbine, red columbine.

Marsh Marigold

Caltha leptosepala

Height: 4–12 in
Leaves: to 2½ in long, 1–3 in wide, basal
Flowers: ¾–1½ in wide, white or greenish
Fruit: up to ¾ in long, beaked, bright yellow-green

This species has a few distinctive, eye-catching characteristics that help to identify it. Marsh marigold has large,
fleshy basal leaves, 5–10 or more showy, white sepals and
many bright yellow-green stamens and pistils clumped in the
center of the flower. • Native peoples in Alaska enjoyed eating many parts of this
species, yet the plant was not so appreciated in our area. **Where found:** marshy
sites in meadows or along streambanks, mountains, wetland-riparian areas and
yellow pine, lodgepole and subalpine forests. **Also known as:** alpine white marsh
marigold.

Buttercup

Ranunculus spp.

Height: ½–2 ft
Leaves: variable, 1–4 in long
Flowers: ½–1 in wide, yellow
Fruit: spherical head of 5–20 tiny achenes

The butter analogy only goes as far as the color, not to any
culinary uses—this plant is poisonous to people and livestock.
However, buttercup essence is popular and is used in holistic
treatments. It is said to help the soul realize its inner light and
beauty. **Where found:** chaparral, montane, grassy slopes, coastal
bluffs, sagebrush scrub and forest openings.

Meadowrue

Thalictrum spp.

Height: 1–5 ft
Leaves: ½–2 in long, divided 3–4 times into 3s
Flowers: sepals <1 inch, petals absent
Fruit: achenes, <1 inch long

These tall, delicate woodland plants produce inconspicuous, greenish
to purplish, male or female flowers without petals. The flowers have
long sepals and either dangling anthers or greenish to purplish,
lance-shaped fruits (achenes) in loose clusters, depending on
the time of year. • The pleasant-smelling plants and seeds were
burned in smudges or stored with possessions as insect repellent
and perfume. Chewed seeds were rubbed onto hair and skin as
perfume. **Where found:** chaparral, foothills, montane and subalpine.

Beach Strawberry

Fragaria chiloensis

Height: to 10 in
Leaves: to 8 in, leathery, 3 leaflets
Flowers: to 1½ in wide, 5–7 petals
Fruit: strawberry, to ½ in wide

There are several species of strawberry in various habitats in our area, always distinguishable by the spreading runners, white flowers and, of course, sweet red fruits. This species, however, is one of the parents of all cultivated strawberries (*F. virginiana* is another and looks very similar). • The fruits of beach strawberry can be made into jams, pies and other sweet treats, but they are tiny and take some patience to collect in quantity and self-control to not simply pop them into one's mouth! **Where found:** sand dunes, sea bluffs and beaches at sea level. **Also known as:** coastal strawberry.

Apache Plume

Fallugia paradoxa

Height: 3–8 ft
Leaves: ¾ in long, evergreen, lobed
Flowers: >1 in across, white
Fruit: showy tassel-like seedheads

The crisp white flowers are fragrant and have a long blooming season in the desert, from April until October. The feathery pink seedheads are the real show stoppers, covering the plant almost year-round. • Early settlers named this plant after the ornate feathered headdresses of the Apache Indians. **Where found:** dry, rocky slopes and flats, desert mountains and Joshua tree and pinyon-juniper woodlands.

Violets

Viola spp.

Height: to 20 in
Leaves: to 2 in wide, heart-shaped
Flowers: ⅝ in long
Fruit: capsules

Violets can be various colors, from the typical violet-blue to white or yellow, often with violet-colored stripes on the lower 3 petals. • Violets are hardy, resistant to most diseases and very prolific. Successful pioneer species in clearings and disturbed sites, they produce numerous brown seeds in explosive capsules and can populate available ground space quickly. **Where found:** moist forests, glades, clearings, streamsides, wetland-riparian areas and yellow pine forests at all elevations.

Broadleaf Lupine

Lupinus polyphyllus

Height: to 5 ft
Leaves: to 5 in long, with 10–17 leaflets
Flowers: ½ in long, in dense clusters 3–16 in long
Fruit: seedpods, to 2 in long

These attractive perennials, with their showy flower clusters and fuzzy seedpods, enrich the soil with nitrogen. • The pods look like hairy garden peas, and children may incorrectly assume that they are edible. Many lupines contain poisonous alkaloids, and it is difficult to distinguish between poisonous and non-poisonous species. • The leaves are silvery hairy, and the pea-like flowers have silky upper sides. **Where found:** wet, open areas, disturbed sites and montane at low to mid elevations.

Clovers

Trifolium spp.

Height: from 1–10 in, depending on the species
Leaves: variable in size depending on the species, divided into 3 leaflets
Flowers: tiny, in dense flowerheads
Fruit: pods, variable in size depending on the species

Clovers are some of the most familiar flowering plants, beloved for their promise of luck to those who find a "leaf of 4." Although clovers are quickly identifiable, they can be quite diverse in color, ranging from white to bright fuchsia, and in size, varying from tiny species that hide in the grass to tall, proud species with lofty leaves. • The flowerheads are actually a tight cluster of small flowers. **Where found:** various grassy habitats, chaparral and montane at low to subalpine elevations; often invasive.

Winter Vetch

Vicia villosa

Height: vine, 2–5 ft long
Leaves: hairy, divided into 5–10 pairs of narrow leaflets, each 1–2 in long, leaf tips with tendrils
Flowers: ¾ in long, in a long-stalked cluster of 10–40 flowers
Fruit: smooth pods, ½–¾ in long

An introduced annual or biennial, this vetch thrives in our climate. It is very hairy overall and often has 2-toned flowers that combine reds or purples with white. East of the Cascades, its abundance is visible, with entire hillsides often tinted purple with these flowers. • Vetch flowers are longer than wide, differentiating them from lupine, wild pea and lotus flowers. **Where found:** chaparral, disturbed sites, roadsides and fields below 3000 ft. **Also known as:** woolly vetch.

187

Fireweed & California Fuschias

Epilobium spp.

Height: variable 2–8 ft
Leaves: ¾–8 in, lance-shaped
Flowers: 1–2 in
Fruit: cylindrical capsule, size varies with species, numerous seeds

Fireweed flowers form in erect clusters and California fuschias (not true fuschias) are trumpet-shaped, but both appear in striking shades of pink, magenta, orange or crimson. Fireweed helps heal landscape scars (e.g., roadsides, burned forests) when seedpods release hundreds of tiny seeds tipped with fluffy, white hairs. Both species paint the landscape with abundant colorful flowers. **Where found:** open, often disturbed sites from desert foothills to montane and subalpine zones, chaparral and coastal sage scrub. **Also known as:** willowherb, hummingbird flower.

Cow Parsnip

Heracleum lanatum

Height: up to 10 ft
Leaves: 6–16 in long, divided into 3 large segments
Flowers: tiny, white, in large, flat-topped clusters up to 1 ft wide
Fruit: oblong, pale tawny carpel with very fine hairs ¼–½ in long

The tiny flowers contrast with the overall largeness of this member of the carrot family (Apiaceae). Even its genus name derives from the great Hercules of Greek mythology. • Cow parsnip can cause skin irritation because it contains phototoxic furanocoumarins that are activated by exposure to sunlight. The plant is edible and was a valuable staple to many Native peoples. Be careful not to confuse it with highly poisonous hemlock species that are similar in appearance. **Where found:** streambanks, moist slopes and clearings, upper beaches and marshes from sea level to subalpine elevations. **Also known as:** *H. sphondylium*.

Northern Gentian

Gentianella amarella

Height: 4–20 in
Leaves: 2 in long, in pairs
Flowers: <1 in long, bluish, tubular
Fruit: capsules

The flowers, about the width of a dime, have petals that range in color from blue or violet-pink to purple and that barely extend past the green sepals. The egg-shaped basal leaves form a cluster and fade early in the season, while the pairs of narrower stem leaves persist. • The genus name *Gentianella* means "little gentian," the plant having been split off from the genus *Gentiana*. **Where found:** moist meadows and clearings at 5000–11,000 ft. **Also known as:** felwort.

Western Waterleaf

Hydrophyllum occidentale

Height: ½–2 ft
Leaves: divided into 7–15 segments, each 1½ in long
Flowers: tiny, lavender, bell-shaped, in clusters
Fruit: ovoid capsules, about ⅛–¼ in wide with 1–3 seeds

The somewhat hairy, somewhat cupped leaves of this plant are adapted to collect and hold a bit of water, hence their name. • The dense inflorescence has a hairy appearance owing to the long stamens and pistils that reach out of the flowers. **Where found:** moist woods, forest openings, yellow pine forests, wetland-riparian areas and foothills to mid-mountain elevations. **Also known as:** California waterleaf.

Baby Blue-eyes

Nemophila menziesii

Height: 4–12 in
Leaves: 1–2 in long, deeply 5–13-lobed
Flowers: 1½ in across, bowl-shaped, blue with white center
Fruit: capsules, ¼–½ in wide

When scattered among the green grass of the foothills in spring, baby blue-eyes wink and capture your own eyes with their beauty. • The species name for this lovely flower honors 18th-century naturalist and explorer Archibald Menzies. **Where found:** chaparral, grassy flats, meadows, forest openings and slopes east of the Sierra Nevada from 50–5000 ft.

Lacy Phacelia

Phacelia tanacetifolia

Height: 12–24 in
Leaves: variable from ¾ to 7¾ in
Flowers: clusters of tiny ¼ in flowers
Fruit: ¼ in capsules of tiny seeds

This native Southern California annual wildflower has naturalized throughout the western United States. The stalk uncurls slowly unwinding as it blooms into a lovely lavender flower with outward radiating stamens, twice as long as the petals. **Where found:** sandy or gravelly slopes, roadsides, gardens, scrublands, yellow pine forests, foothill woodlands, chaparral, valley grasslands, creosote bush scrub; the Mojave Desert. **Also known as:** purple tansy.

Spreading Phlox

Phlox diffusa

Height: 2–4 in
Leaves: ¼–¾ in long, paired
Flowers: ½–¾ in wide, white, pink or bluish, solitary
Fruit: 3-chambered capsule

This phlox gets its name for its beautiful way of pouring over rocks in low, loose mats that carpet the ground with dense greenery or, when in bloom, blankets of brightly colored flowers. Each sweet-smelling blossom is a pinwheel-like fan of 5 petals fused at their bases into a tube ⅜–⅝ in long. **Where found:** open, rocky outcrops, slopes and scree, and open forests from low montane to above treeline.

Toothed Downingia

Downingia cuspidata

Height: 2–6 in
Leaves: ¼–½ in long, narrow
Flowers: ¼–½ in long, blue to lavender with a white center and a yellow spot
Fruit: capsule, 1¼–2¾ in long

This member of the bluebell family (Campanulaceae) usually has bright blue flowers but also occurs with very pale lavender or almost white variations. However, the blossoms always have a large, yellow spot, which can be slightly divided into 2 spots, at the base of the lower corolla lip. The top 2 petals are very narrow and stick up like rabbit's ears. **Where found:** below 1600 ft in chaparral, dried mud bottoms of vernal pools and wet meadows.

Pennyroyal

Monardella odoratissima

Height: 1½–2 ft
Leaves: ¼–1¾ in long, in pairs
Flowers: ⅜–½ in long, whitish to pale purple or pink, in terminal clusters
Fruit: oblong nutlets

This plant's strong scent will leave no doubt that it is a mint, and its flavor is so strong that even cold water will become infused. In addition, the square stem is a telltale characteristic of members of the mint family (Lamiaceae). • The flowerheads are composed of many small flowers with long bracts and protruding stamens, and these plants typically grow in crowded masses, filling areas with color and fragrance. **Where found:** dry slopes, sagebrush scrub and montane forests. **Also known as:** mountain monardella, coyote mint.

Woolly Bluecurls

Trichostema lanatum

Height: 3–5 ft
Leaves: 1½–3 in
Flowers: 12 in fuzzy spikes, blue, pink or white
Fruit: 2–4 nutlets, <⅛ in

The fuzzy, colorful flowers of woolly bluecurls punctuate their beauty with long extended stamens that stick out like exclamation points. They not only attract our attention but also that of butterflies, bees and hummingbirds. These plants have a long blooming season, and the evergreen leaves keep color on the landscape year-round. **Where found:** Sonoran Desert washes and flats, dry slopes, Peninsular Range, chaparral, creosote bush scrub and Joshua tree woodlands.

White Sage

Salvia apiana

Height: 2–4 ft
Leaves: 1–3 in
Flowers: 1 in, tube-shaped, white
Fruit: nutlets, shiny, light brown, <⅛ in

This aromatic evergreen has white densely hairy leaves and spike-like clusters of tube-shaped white flowers on 4-ft stalks. • This plant has many ethnobotanical properties used for culinary, medicinal and spiritual purposes. It was used in sweat lodges as a smudge, or more recently as a sort of incense that cleanses the air while wild stocks of the plant are being unsustainably harvested to stock New Age gift shops. Black sage *(S. melifera)* is common in more moist habitats of Southern California but is considered inferior in quality to white sage. **Where found:** dry slopes, coastal Peninsular Range, coastal sage scrub, deserts and chaparral. **Also known as:** bee sage, sacred sage.

Scarlet Paintbrush

Castilleja miniata

Height: 8–24 in
Leaves: 2–2¾ in long
Flowers: ¾–1¼ in long, greenish, tubular, concealed by hairy, red bracts
Fruit: 2-celled capsules

It is usually easy to recognize a paintbrush, but *Castilleja* is a confusing genus, with many flower shapes and colors, and species that often hybridize. • Paintbrushes have poor photosynthetic abilities and partially parasitize nearby plants to steal nutrients. • Showy, leaf-like bracts give these flower clusters their red color. The actual flowers are the tubular, greenish blossoms concealed within the bracts. **Where found:** open woods and meadows, grassy slopes, tidal marshes, disturbed sites, wetland-riparian areas, montane and yellow pine, and lodgepole and subalpine forests. **Also known as:** common red paintbrush, giant paintbrush, great red paintbrush.

Yellow Monkeyflower

Mimulus guttatus

Height: 4–20 in
Leaves: ½–2 in long, in pairs
Flowers: ½–1⅝ in long, yellow, trumpet-shaped
Fruit: oblong capsules, ½–¾ in long

This snapdragon brightens streamsides, rocky seeps and wet ditches. • *Mimulus* is the diminutive form of the Latin *mimus*, meaning "a buffoon or actor in a farce or mime." The common name also alludes to the fancied resemblance of this flower to a small, grinning, ape-like face. • This variable species often roots from nodes or sends out stolons. **Where found:** wet sites in foothills, montane and subalpine zones. **Also known as:** seep monkeyflower.

Penstemon

Penstemon spp.

Height: 1–6 ft
Leaves: oval to lance-shaped, typically larger towards the base, varying in size up to 3 in long
Flowers: 1–2 in long, tubular
Fruit: small capsules, <½ in

Among the 90 or so species and varieties of penstemon in California is a diversity of color ranging from blue, purple or pink to red, orange and white, and these members of the snapdragon family vary in height from barely knee-high to over your head. The 5 petals unite into long, 2-lipped tubes that stand out like loud colorful trumpets, and the woolly throats and anthers add to the interest of these showy flowers. **Where found:** from low desert to alpine meadows and rocky ridges near and above treeline; widespread. **Also known as:** beard tongue.

American Brooklime

Veronica americana

Height: 4–27½ in
Leaves: to 2 in long
Flowers: ¼ in wide, saucer-shaped
Fruit: round capsules, ⅛ in long

The leaves of American brooklime are edible and are commonly used in salads or as a potherb. Because this plant most often grows directly in water, be sure not to collect the leaves from plants in polluted sites. • The showy flowers are blue to violet, sometimes white, with red-purple markings and 2 large, reaching stamens that look like antennae. **Where found:** wetland-riparian areas and shallow water alongside slow-moving streams, springs, marshes, seepage areas, wet meadows, clearings and ditches at low to mid elevations. **Also known as:** American speedwell.

Common Yarrow

Achillea millefolium

Height: 4–31 in
Leaves: 1¼–4 in long, fern-like
Flowers: <¼ in wide, white or pinkish with cream-colored centers, in clusters
Fruit: hairless, flattened achenes

This hardy, aromatic perennial has served for thousands of years as a fumigant, insecticide and medicine. The Greek hero Achilles, for whom the genus was named, supposedly used it to heal his soldiers' wounds after battle. • Yarrow is also an attractive ornamental, but beware—its extensive underground stems (rhizomes) can soon invade your garden. **Where found:** chaparral and dry to moist, open sites from plains to alpine zones.

Leafy Aster

Symphyotrichum foliaceum

Height: ½–3 ft
Leaves: 2–6 in long
Flowers: ray flowers ⅓–¾ in long; disk flowers tiny, yellow
Fruit: hairy achenes

One of the loveliest flowers in our area is also one of the most common. The yellow disk flowers in the center of the inflorescence are surrounded by ray flowers that can range in color from white to blue, pink, purple or red. Directly below the inflorescence is a collar of many green, leafy bracts that stick out perpendicular to the stem. **Where found:** open woods, meadows and streambanks from mid to high elevations.

Brass Buttons

Cotula coronopifolia

Height: 8–16 in
Leaves: ⅜–1⅜ in long, narrow
Flowers: ¼–½ in wide, yellow, rays absent
Fruit: achenes

True to their name, the showy, bright yellow, disk-shaped flower-heads of this plant look like shiny brass buttons, and they are also pleasantly aromatic. • Brass buttons is a South African species introduced to our area, as well as to many other parts of the world, where it typically colonizes beaches. It is very salt tolerant but also brightens up brackish, muddy, non-coastal sites. **Where found:** along the coast and near inland vernal pools, chaparral, beaches, tidal mudflats, marshes, salt marshes and estuaries. **Also known as:** mud disk, golden buttons, buttonweed.

Fleabane

Erigeron spp.

Height: 4–28 in
Leaves: ½–8 in long, reduced in size upwards along the stem
Flowers: ray flowers 30–80, pink or purplish; disk flowers yellow; in heads ½–2 in wide
Fruit: hairy, ribbed achenes with hair-like parachutes, <¼ in

Fleabanes, a type of daisy, are easily confused with asters. Aster flowerheads usually have overlapping rows of bracts with light, parchment-like bases and green tips. Fleabanes usually have 1 row of slender bracts with the same texture and color (not green) throughout. Also, fleabanes generally flower earlier and have narrower, more numerous rays. **Where found:** various habitats from wetland-riparian, sandy slopes and beaches to open sites in foothills to alpine zones; seaside daisy *(E. glaucus)* is common in the coastal sage scrub.

Common Tarweed

Madia elegans

Height: 1–3 ft
Leaves: ¾–8 in long
Flowers: ray flowers ⅜–⅝ in long, yellow; disk flowers yellow; in heads 1–1½ in wide
Fruit: achenes

The long, golden, petal-like ray flowers are often 2-toned, with either white or dark red to maroon at the base. • The name "tarweed" refers to the plant's sticky, black, glandular hairs, which readily adhere to skin and clothing upon contact. The fragrance of tarweed is also heavy and sticky, almost tar-like. **Where found:** chaparral and grassy fields below 3000 ft. **Also known as:** common madia, elegant tarweed.

Woolly Mule Ears

Wyethia mollis

Height: 10–20 in
Leaves: 8–16 in long, gray-green, mostly basal
Flowers: ray flowers 5–20, yellow; disk flowers yellow; in heads up to 4 in wide
Fruit: achenes, ⅜ in long

Large masses of woolly mule ears often cover mid-elevation meadows, indicating that the hillside they are growing on is most likely of volcanic origin. The long roots of this species can reach deep into the porous volcanic soil to find water that other plants cannot access. • The name "mule ears" refers to this plant's relatively large leaves, which grow upward. The plant's dense woolly hairs and leaf growth formation help reduce water loss. **Where found:** montane and open slopes at 4000–10,500 ft. **Also known as:** narrow-leaved mule ears.

Goldenrod

Solidago spp.

Height: 1–6 ft
Leaves: 2–4 in long, alternate, lance-shaped, sharply toothed
Flowers: <¼ in wide, yellow, clustered in a terminal spike
Fruit: oblong hairy akene, <¼ in

Ten species of goldenrod are native to California, with diverse habitat preferences and ranging as far north as Canada. The bold, pyramid-shaped flower clusters are among the most conspicuous late-summer and fall wildflowers and are perceived by many to cause hay fever, but the pollen is actually too heavy to be carried by the wind; instead, it is carried by flying insects. Each seed-like fruit is tipped with parachutes of white hairs. **Where found:** valley grasslands, coastal prairie, chaparral, foothill woodlands and yellow pine forests; widespread throughout California.

Sulphur Buckwheat

Eriogonum umbellatum

Height: 1–4 ft
Leaves: ½–1¼ in, evergreen
Flowers: <⅛ in, yellow, in ball-like clusters atop 4–12 in stalks
Fruit: 3-sided achene

Small rodents and chipmunks feast on the seeds, whereas butterflies and caterpillars go after the flowers and leaves, and deer and sheep graze on the entire plant. This mat-forming perennial has gray-woolly leaves (at least beneath), which become bright red in fall. The flowers are bright sulphur-yellow, often pink-tinged, fading to orange. **Where found:** pinyon-juniper and foothill woodlands, coastal sage scrub, montane, alpine fellfields and yellow pine and lodgepole forests.

195

Bracken Fern

Pteridium aquilinum

Height: up to 10 ft
Leaves: 1–3 ft long, triangular leaves with 10 or more leaflets

This widespread species is common around the world and occurs in a wide variety of habitats, though in our area, it prefers open or disturbed sites. • The deep rhizomes spread easily and help the plant survive fires. • Native peoples used the fronds to line pit ovens and ate the rhizomes. **Where found:** meadows, disturbed sites, clearings, dry to wet forests, lakeshores and bogs from low to subalpine elevations.

Sword Fern

Polystichum munitum

Height: up to 5 ft
Leaves: up to 40 in long, 2½–8½ in wide, lance-shaped, with numerous leaflets

Plants in the genus *Polystichum* are large, tufted, evergreen ferns that form crown-like bunches from a single woody rhizome. The sword fern is one of several *Polystichum* species in our area. • This plant was used by Native peoples for lining pit ovens, wrapping and storing food, flooring and bedding. • This fern has large, circular sori and as many as 75–100 fronds. **Where found:** chaparral and yellow pine forests from low to mid elevations.

Maidenhair Fern

Adiantum pedatum

Height: up to 2 ft
Leaves: 6–24 in across and almost as long, palmate, compound, with numerous leaflets

Though it grows in colonies and can appear lush, this delicate fern typically has a single or very few palmately branched leaves on thin, dark brown or purple-black stems. • This fern was often used in Native basketry as well as medicinally. It was also exported to Europe and used in herbal cough medicines. **Where found:** chaparral, foothill woodlands, forests, alongside streams and waterfalls, and in shady, humus-rich sites, from low to mid elevations. **Also known as:** *A. aleuticum*.

Desert Agave

Agave deserti

Height: 1–3 ft
Leaves: 2–3 ft long
Flowers: yellow clusters atop 6–15 ft stalks

This classic desert plant lives for 8–25 years before it sends up an impressively tall flowering stalk, like a flag announcing the final salutation of the plant—after the yellow flowers bloom and then fade, the plant itself also dies. • Desert agave grows 2–6 ft wide, so that the plant is generally wider than it is tall. • Many western and Mexican species of agave exist in the wild, and several more cultivars grow in gardens and botanical parks. • Tequila is distilled from this plant, and agave nectar is used as a sweetener similar to honey. **Where found:** creosote bush scrub, coastal sage scrub, desert flats and sandy, gravely hills and slopes. **Also known as:** century plant.

Prickly Pear Cactus

Opuntia littoralis

Height: 3 ft
Flowers: yellow to red, 1–1½ in wide
Fruit: dark red to purple juicy "pears," 1–2 in, oval
Spines: 1–2 in

The pads of the prickly pear cactus are covered in clusters of tiny, hair-like barbed thorns that cause extreme discomfort if they get into your skin. Despite this risk, cactus pads and the sweet fruits are used in Mexican cuisine. • This hardy cactus grows to 15 ft wide, significantly wider than it is tall. It thrives in full sun but is also tolerant of cool desert temperatures down to -10° F. **Where found:** coastal sage scrub, chaparral, desert, ridges and hillsides; throughout arid regions of Southern California, including the Channel Islands.

Winterfat

Krascheninnikovia lanata

Height: 1–3 ft
Leaves: ½–1½ in long, crowded, bluish green, evergreen with white or rust-colored star-shaped hairs making the leaves look woolly
Flowers: small, silvery white, woolly and inconspicuous with no petals, but form plumes of fluffy white seedheads that cover the plant
Fruit: showy, cottony seedheads, ⅕–⅓ in long, cover the entire plant making the branches look like long, woolly plumes

The showy stems and fluffy seedheads make this plant popular in ornamental gardens and dried flower arrangements. It is also an important wildlife plant, providing forage for many species, such as mule deer, bighorn sheep, rabbits and ground squirrels that rely on it when other plants have expired. **Where found:** creosote bush scrub, pinyon-juniper woodlands and dry desert soils. **Also known as:** *Ceratoides lanata; Eurotia lanata.*

197

Sea Grasses (Surf Grass & Eel Grass)

Phyllospadix spp. and *Zostera* spp.

Length: up to 10 ft

Not algae and not grass, sea grasses are flowering plants that are truly marine, spending almost their entire lives underwater, rarely exposed at low tide, when long, narrow, bright green strands can be seen in shallow, rocky waters.
• Sea grass flowers are tiny and inconspicuous because there is no need to attract insects for pollination. Pollen is released in long, thread-like strands and carried by water currents. The seeds are dispersed by water or fish. **Where found:** low intertidal and subtidal zones; eel grass prefers soft substrate in sheltered areas; surf grass requires rocky coasts with considerable wave action.

Turkish Towel · Red Algae

Gigartina exasperata

Length: up to 6 ft

Most marine plants are algae—lacking flowers, leaves or roots. There are 3 types of algae along California's coast: green, brown and red. Turkish towel is among the most massive of the red algae species. Red algae are the largest group of seaweeds. They are the most abundant and comprise most species of seaweed in the world. Two of the most notable along the California coast include nori (*Porphyra* spp., cultivated in East Asia and routinely used in Japanese cooking) and Turkish towel. • A red pigment typically masks the chlorophyll that would otherwise render these algae green in color. **Where found:** intertidal and low, subtidal zones.

Giant Kelp · Brown Algae

Macrocystis spp.

Length: up to 330 ft

Macrocystis pyrifera is the most admired brown algae and is the foundation for the entire marine ecosystem. It is particularly suited to the cold Pacific waters. • Giant kelp is the largest and fastest growing plant in the marine environment. The entire frond is able to photosynthesize and, under ideal conditions, this plant is able to grow up to 2 ft in a single day. • Kelp forests are among the most biodiverse forests, including terrestrial ones, in the world. **Where found:** in waters 50–68° F, on rocky substrate where the plant can attach.

Bull Kelp · Brown Algae

Nereocystis luetkeana

Length: 30–60 ft; up to 115 ft

Bull kelp forests provide habitat and shelter for a myriad of marine life—sea otters wrap themselves up in bull kelp that is adhered to the ocean floor so that they can take a nap without drifting away. • Bull kelp is hollow with a bulbous float at the top and is filled with gasses that are 10% carbon monoxide. **Where found:** attached to rocky substrates; populations are increasingly abundant north of San Francisco Bay.

Sea Lettuce · Green Algae

Ulva lactuca

Length: 7 in

There are few green algae species found in the intertidal zone, but the most visible and abundant is the bright green sea lettuce, which either attaches to rocks or is free-floating. • This algae has a very simple structure that is only 2 cells thick. • Sea lettuce has a high caloric value and is eaten by crabs and mollusks. **Where found:** shallow bays, lagoons, harbors, marshes and on rocks and other algae in intertidal and high-tide zones.

199

REFERENCES

Acorn, John, and Ian Sheldon. 2002. *Bugs of Northern California*. Lone Pine Publishing, Edmonton, AB.

Bailey, Robert G. 1995. 2nd edition. Descriptions of the Ecoregions of the United States. United States Department of Agriculture Forest Service, Washington D.C. http://www.fs.fed.us/rm/analytics/publications/ecoregionsindex.html. Accessed July 2007.

Bailey, Robert G. 1995. 2nd edition. Descriptions of the Ecoregions of the United States. United States Department of Agriculture Forest Service, Washington D.C. http://www.fs.fed.us/rm/analytics/staff/Bailey.html. Accessed July 2007.

Bezener, Andy, and Linda Kershaw. 1999. *Rocky Mountain Nature Guide*. Lone Pine Publishing, Edmonton, AB.

Blackwell, Laird R. 1999. *Wildflowers of the Sierra Nevada and the Central Valley*. Lone Pine Publishing, Edmonton, AB.

California Reptiles and Amphibians. http://www.californiaherps.com/index.html. Accessed August 2008.

California Sate Parks. California Department of Parks and Recreation. http://www.parks.ca.gov/?page_id=21491. Accessed September 2008.

Complete List of Amphibians, Reptile, Bird and Mammal Species in California, California Department of Fish and Game. http://www.dfg.ca.gov/bdb/pdfs/species_list.pdf. Accessed August 2008.

National Park Service. US Department of the Interior. http://home.nps.gov/applications/parksearch/state.cfm?st=CA. Accessed September 2008.

Eder, Tamara. 2002. *Whales and other Marine Mammals of California and Baja.* Lone Pine Publishing, Edmonton, AB.

Eder, Tamara. 2005. *Mammals of Northern California.* Lone Pine Publishing, Edmonton, AB.

Fisher, Chris C., and Herbert Clarke. 1997. *Birds of San Diego.* Lone Pine Publishing, Edmonton, AB.

Fisher, Chris C., and Herbert Clarke. 1997. *Birds of Los Angeles, including Santa Barbara, Ventura and Orange Counties.* Lone Pine Publishing, Edmonton, AB.

Fix, David, and Andy Bezener. 2000. *Birds of Northern California.* Lone Pine Publishing, Edmonton, AB.

Jepson, Willis Linn. 1909. *Trees of California.* Cunningham, Curtis and Welch, San Francisco, CA.

Leatherwood, Stephen, and Randall R. Reeves. 1983. *The Sierra Club Handbook of Whales and Dolphins.* Sierra Club Books, San Francisco, CA.

Miller, George Oxford. 2008. *Landscaping with Native Plants of Southern California.* Voyageur Press, St. Paul, NM.

National Audubon Society. 1998. *Field Guide to North American Seashore Creatures.* Chanticleer Press, Toronto, ON.

National Audubon Society. 1998. *Field Guide to North American Fishes, Whales & Dolphins.* Chanticleer Press, Toronto, ON.

Sheldon, Ian. 1998. *Animal Tracks of Southern California.* Lone Pine Publishing, Edmonton, AB.

Sheldon, Ian. 2007. *Seashore of Southern California.* Lone Pine Publishing, Edmonton, AB.

Snyderman, Marty. 1998. *California Marine Life: a guide to common marine species.* Roberts Rinehart, Niwot, CO.

St. John, Alan. 2002. *Reptiles of the Northwest, California to Alaska Rockies to the Coast.* Lone Pine Publishing, Edmonton, AB.

GLOSSARY

A

achene: a seed-like fruit, e.g., sunflower seed

algae: simple photosynthetic aquatic plants lacking true stems, roots, leaves and flowers, and ranging in size from single-celled forms to giant kelp

altricial: animals that are helpless at birth or hatching

anadromous: fish that migrate from salt water to fresh water to spawn

annual: plants that live for only 1 year or growing season

anterior: situated at or toward the front

aquatic: water frequenting

arboreal: tree frequenting

arthropod: joint-limbed organisms with hard exoskeletons; from the phylum Arthropoda, which includes crustaceans, centipedes, insects and spiders

autotrophic: an organism that produces its own food, e.g., by photosynthesis

B

barbels: fleshy, whisker-like appendages found on some fish

basal leaf: a leaf arising from the base of a plant

bajada: convergence of several alluvial fans, creating a broad slope of debris deposited by streams down the lower slopes of mountains; typical of semi-arid climates

benthic: bottom feeding

berry: a fleshy fruit, usually with several to many seeds

bivalve: a group of mollusks in which the animal is enclosed by 2 valves (shells)

bract: a leaf-like structure arising from the base of a flower or inflorescence

bracteole: a small bract borne on a leaf stalk

brood parasite: a bird that parasitizes other bird's nests by laying its eggs and then abandoning them for the parasitized birds to raise, e.g., brown-headed cowbird

bulb: a fleshy underground organ with overlapping, swollen scales, e.g., an onion

C

calyx: a collective term for the sepals of a flower

cambium: inner layers of tissue that transport nutrients up and down the plant stalk or trunk

canopy: the fairly continuous cover provided by the branches and leaves of adjacent trees

capsules: a dry fruit that splits open to release seeds

carapace: a protective bony shell (e.g., of a turtle) or exoskeleton (e.g., of beetles)

carnivorous: feeding primarily on meat

carrion: decomposing animal matter or carcass

catkin: a spike of small flowers

chaparral: low elevation dry scrub dwarf forest, found only in Southern California and northern Mexico; a mature chaparral forest reaches decadence well within a century and is fire dependant for regeneration

chelipeds: the clawed first pair of legs, e.g., on a crab

cismontane: geographical term for the coastal side of the Transverse and Peninsular mountain ranges that divides southern California in half from west to east

compound leaf: a leaf separated into 2 or more divisions called leaflets

cone: the fruit produced by a coniferous plant, composed of overlapping scales round a central axis

coniferous: cone-bearing; seed (female) and pollen (male) cones are borne on the same tree in different locations

corm: a swollen underground stem base used by some plants as an organ of propagation; resembles a bulb

crepuscular: active primarily at dusk and dawn

cryptic coloration: a coloration pattern designed to conceal an animal

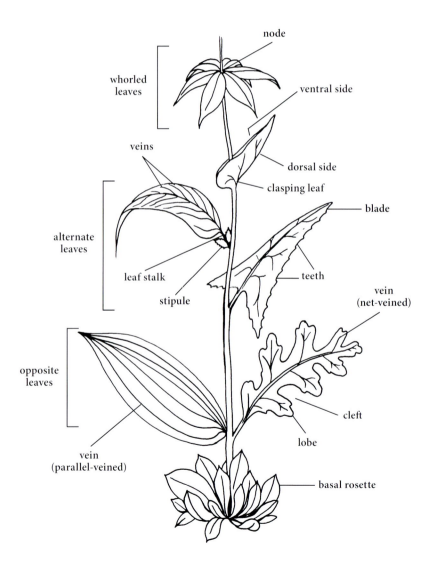

D

deciduous: a tree whose leaves turn color and are shed annually

defoliating: dropping of the leaves

disk flower: a small flower in the center, or disk, of a composite flower (e.g., aster, daisy or sunflower)

diurnal: active primarily during the day

dorsal: the top or back

drupe: a fleshy fruit with a stony pit, e.g., peach, cherry

E

echolocation: navigation by rebounding sound waves off objects to target or avoid them

ecological niche: an ecological role filled by a species

ecoregion: distinction between regions based upon geology, climate, biodiversity, elevation and soil composition

ectoparasites: skin parasites

ectotherm: an animal that regulates its body temperature behaviorally from external sources of heat, i.e., from the sun

eft: the stage of a newt's life following the tadpole stage, in which it exits the water and leads a terrestrial life; when the newt matures to adulthood it returns to the water

endemic: a species with a distribution that is geographically restricted to a limited area or region

endotherm: an animal that regulates its body temperature internally

estivate: a state of inactivity and a slowing of the metabolism to permit survival in extended periods of high temperatures and inadequate water supply

estuarine: an area where a freshwater river exits into the sea; the salinity of the seawater drops because it is diluted by the fresh water

eutrophic: a nutrient-rich body of water with an abundance of algae growth and a low level of dissolved oxygen

evergreen: having green leaves through winter; not deciduous

exoskeleton: a hard outer encasement that provides protection and points of attachment for muscles

F

flight membrane: the membrane between the fore and hind limbs of bats and some squirrels that allows bats to fly and squirrels to glide through the air

follicle: the structure in the skin from which hair or feathers grow; a dry fruit that splits open along a single line on one side when ripe; a cocoon

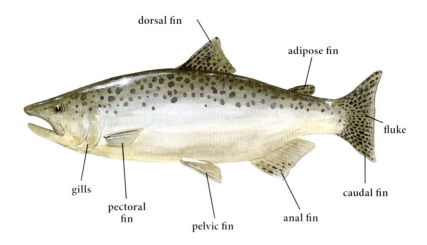

dorsal fin

adipose fin

fluke

gills

pectoral
fin

pelvic fin

anal fin

caudal fin

food web: the elaborated, interconnected feeding relationships of living organisms in an ecosystem

forb: a broad-leaved plant that lacks a permanent woody stem and loses its aboveground growth each year; may be annual, biennial or perennial

G

gillrakers: long, thin, fleshy projections that protect delicate gill tissue from particles in the water

glandular: similar to or containing glands

H

habitat: the physical area in which an organism lives

hawking: feeding behavior in which a bird leaves a perch, snatches its prey in mid-air, and then returns to its previous perch

herbaceous: feeding primarily on vegetation

hibernation: a state of decreased metabolism and body temperature and slowed heart and respiratory rates to permit survival during long periods of cold temperature and diminished food supply

hibernaculum: a shelter in which an animal, usually a mammal, reptile or insect, chooses to hibernate

hips: the berry-like fruit of some plants in the rose family (Rosaceae)

holdfast: the root-like structure that seaweeds use to hold onto rocky substrates

hybrids: the offspring from a cross between parents belonging to different varieties or subspecies, sometimes between different subspecies or genera

I

incubate: to keep eggs at a relatively constant temperature until they hatch

inflorescence: a cluster of flowers on a stalk; may be arranged as a spike, raceme, head, panicle, etc.

insectivorous: feeding primarily on insects

intertidal zone: the area between low- and high-tide lines

invertebrate: any animal lacking a backbone, e.g., worms, slugs, crayfish, shrimps

involucral bract: one of several bracts that form a whorl below a flower or flower cluster

K

key: a winged fruit, usually of an ash or maple; also called a "samara"

L

larva: immature forms of an animal that differ from the adult

leaflet: a division of a compound leaf

lenticel: a slightly raised portion of bark where the cells are packed more loosely, allowing for gas exchange with the atmosphere

lobate: having each toe individually webbed

lobe: a projecting part of a leaf or flower, usually rounded

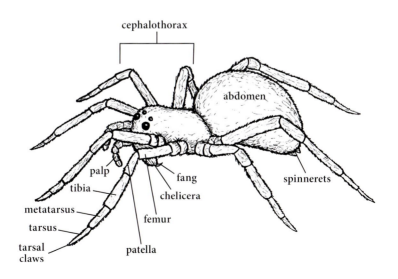

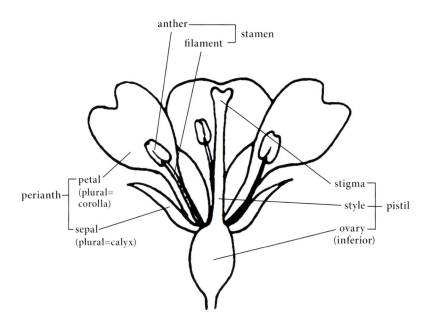

M

metabolic rate: the rate of chemical processes in an organism

metamorphosis: the developmental transformation of an animal from larval to sexually mature adult stage

midden: the pile of cone scales found on the territories of tree squirrels, usually under a favorite tree

molt: when an animal sheds old feathers, fur or skin, to replace them with new growth

montane: of mountainous regions

myccorhizal fungi: fungi that has a mutually beneficial relationship with the roots of some seed plants

N

neotropical migrant: a bird that nests in North America, but overwinters in the New World tropics

nocturnal: active primarily at night

node: a slightly enlarged section of a stem where leaves or branches originate

nudibranch: sea slug

nutlet: a small, hard, single-seeded fruit that remains closed

O

omnivorous: feeding on both plants and animals

ovoid: egg-shaped

P

palmate: leaflets, lobes or veins arranged around a single point, like the fingers on a hand (e.g., maple leaf)

pappus: the modified calyx of composite flowers (e.g., asters or daisies), consisting of awns, scales or bristles at the apex of the achene

parasite: a relationship between 2 species in which one benefits at the expense of the other

patagium: skin forming a flight membrane

pelage: the fur or hair of mammals

perennial: a plant that lives for several years

petal: a member of the inside ring of modified flower leaves, usually brightly colored or white

phenology: stages of growth as influenced by climate

photosynthesis: conversion of CO_2 and water into sugars via energy of the sun

pinniped: a marine mammal with limbs that are modified to form flippers; a seal, sea-lion or walrus

pioneer species: a plant species that is capable of colonizing an otherwise unvegetated area; one of the first species to take hold in a disturbed area

piscivorous: fish-eating

pishing: a noise made to attract birds

pistil: the female organ of a flower, usually consisting of an ovary, style and stigma

plastic species: a species that can adapt to a wide range of conditions

plastron: the lower part of a turtle or tortoise shell, which covers the abdomen

poikilothermic: having a body temperature that is the same as the external environment and varies with it

pollen: the tiny grains produced in a plant's anthers and which contain the male reproductive cells

pollen cone: male cone that produces pollen

polyandry: a mating strategy in which one female mates with several males

pome: a fruit with a core, e.g., apple

precocial: animals who are active and independent at birth or hatching

prehensile: able to grasp

proboscis: the elongated tubular and flexible mouthpart of many insects

R

ray flower: in a composite flower (e.g., aster, daisy or sunflower), a type of flower usually with long, colorful petals that collectively make up the outer ring of petals (the center of a composite flower is composed of disk flowers)

redd: spawing nest for fish

resinous: bearing resin, usually causing stickiness

rhinopores: tentacle-like sensory structures on the head of a nudibranch (sea slug)

rhizome: a horizontal underground stem

rictal bristles: hair-like feathers found on the faces of some birds

riparian: on the bank of a river or other watercourse

rookery: a colony of nests

runner: a slender stolon or prostrate stem that roots at the nodes or the tip

S

samara: a dry, winged fruit with usually only a single seed (e.g., maple or ash); also called a "key"

salmonid: a member of the Salmonidae family of fishes; includes trout, char, salmon, whitefish and grayling

sclerophyllic: tolerant of a climate with high temperatures and low humidity; sclerophyllic plants have tough, leathery evergreen foliage

scutes: individual plates on a turtle's shell

seed cone: female cone that produces seeds

sepal: the outer, usually green, leaf-like structures that protect the flower bud and are located at the base of an open flower

silicle: a fruit of the mustard family (Brassicaceae) that is 2-celled and usually short, wide and often flat

silique: a long, thin fruit with many seeds; characteristic of some members of the mustard family (Brassicaceae)

sorus (pl. sori): a collection of sporangia under a fern frond; in some lichens and fungi, a structure that produces pores

spadix: a fleshy spike with many small flowers

spathe: a leaf-like sheath that surrounds a spadix

spur: a pointed projection

stamen: the pollen-bearing organ of a flower

stigma: a receptive tip in a flower that receives pollen

stolon: a long branch or stem that runs along the ground and often propagates more plants

subnivean: below the surface of the snow

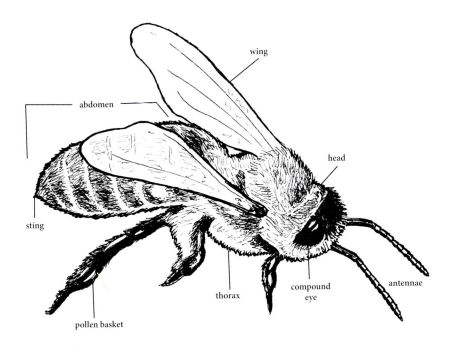

substrate: the surface that an organism grows on; the material that makes up a streambed (e.g., sand or gravel)

suckering: a method of tree and shrub reproduction in which shoots arise from an underground stem

syrinx: a bird's vocal organ

T

taproot: the main, large root of a plant from which smaller roots arise, e.g., carrot

tendril: a slender, clasping or twining outgrowth from a stem or a leaf

terrestrial: land frequenting

torpor: a state of physical inactivity

tragus: a prominent structure of the outer ear of a bat

tubercule: a round nodule or warty outgrowth

tubular flower: a type of flower in which all or some of the petals are fused together at the base

tundra: a high-altitude ecological zone at the northernmost limits of plant growth, where plants are reduced to shrubby or mat-like growth

tympanum: eardrum; the hearing organ of a frog

U

ungulate: an animal that has hooves

V

ventral: of or on the abdomen (belly)

vermiculations: wavy-patterned makings

vertebrate: an animal possessing a backbone

vibrissae: bristle-like feathers growing around the beak of birds to aid in catching insects

W

whorl: a circle of leaves or flowers around a stem

woolly: bearing long or matted hairs

INDEX

Names in **boldface** type indicate primary species.

INDEX

222

ABOUT THE AUTHOR

Erin McCloskey spent her formative years observing nature from atop her horse. She used to watch the great migrations of birds in autumn flying over the harvested wheat fields on their way south for the winter—one day she would follow them. Today she lives in Southern California, where she enjoys the nature as well as the climate! Erin received her BSc with distinction in environmental and conservation sciences, majoring in conservation biology and management. An active campaigner for the protection of endangered species and spaces, Erin has collaborated with various NGOs and has been involved in numerous conservation projects around the world. Currently, she is based in Los Angeles as the North American operations manager for Biosphere Expeditions, an organization that runs scientific research expeditions in support of wildlife conservation worldwide. Erin began working as an editor in 1996. From 2000–05, she lived in Italy, where she freelanced as a writer and editor for several magazine and book publishers focused on nature, travel, scientific research and even alternative healthcare. Erin is the author of *The Bradt Travel Guide to Argentina*, *Ireland Flying High*, *Canada Flying High*, *Hawaii from the Air* and co-author/editor for the *Green Volunteers* guidebook series. Erin is also the author of the *Washington and Oregon Nature Guide*, the *Northern California Nature Guide* and *Bear Attacks*.